DONALD J. TRUMP
45TH PRESIDENT OF THE UNITED STATES
Coloring Book

Illustrated by S. Eileen Montaño

This book is for entertainment purposes only.

All quotes by Donald J. Trump

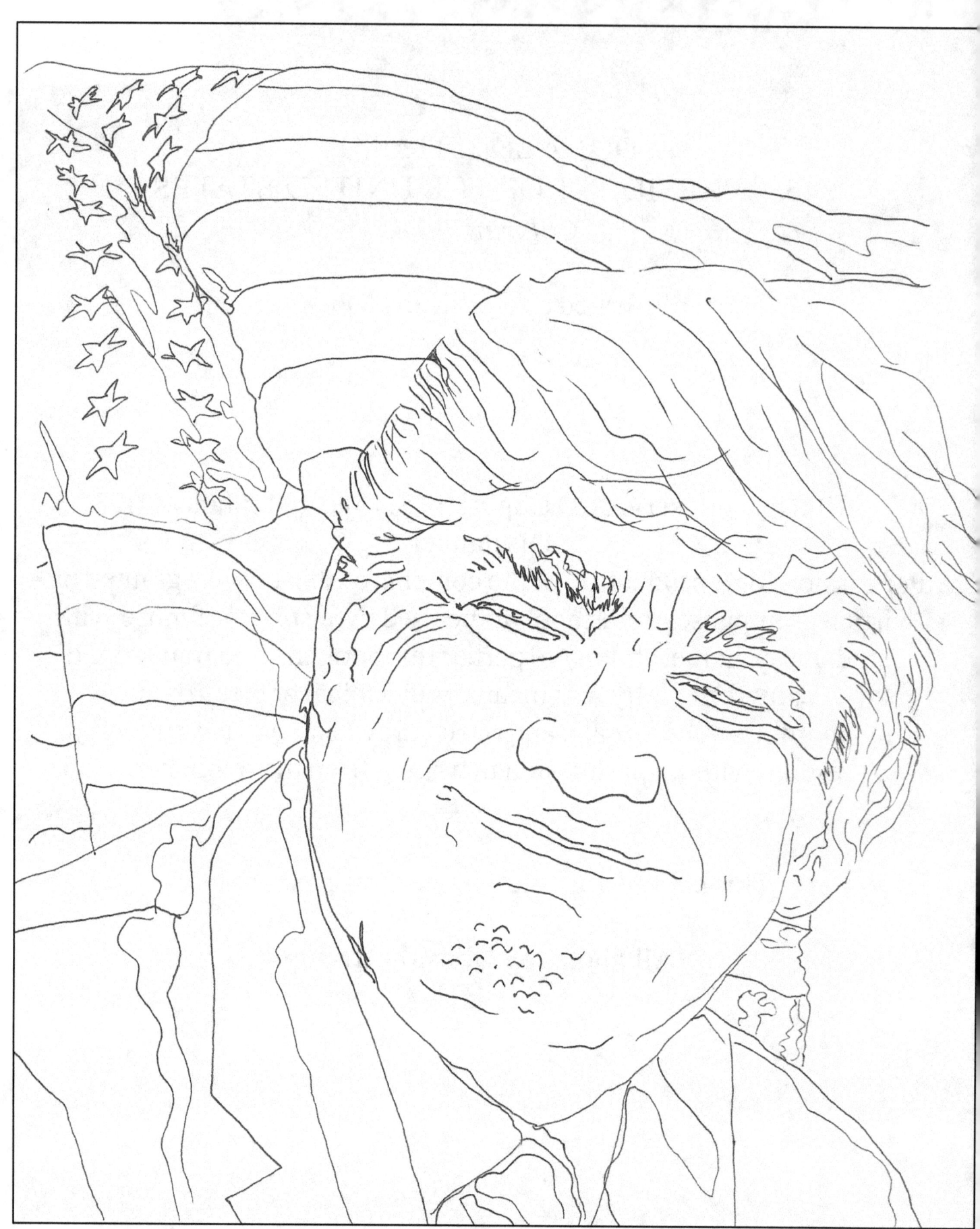

"Happy Cinco de Mayo! The best taco bowls are made in
Trump Tower Grill. I love Hispanics!"

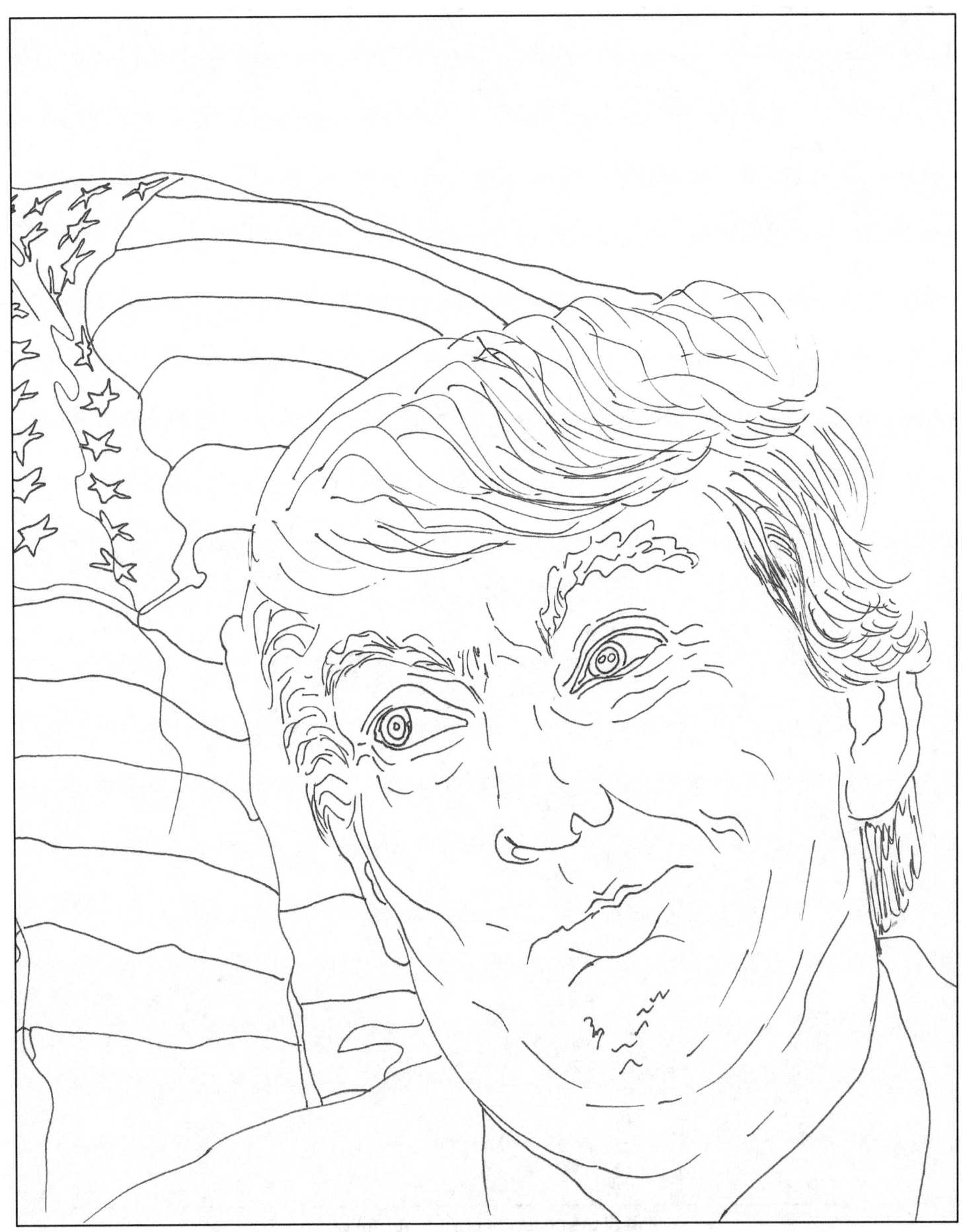

"All of the women on The Apprentice flirted with me - consciously or unconsciously.
That's to be expected."

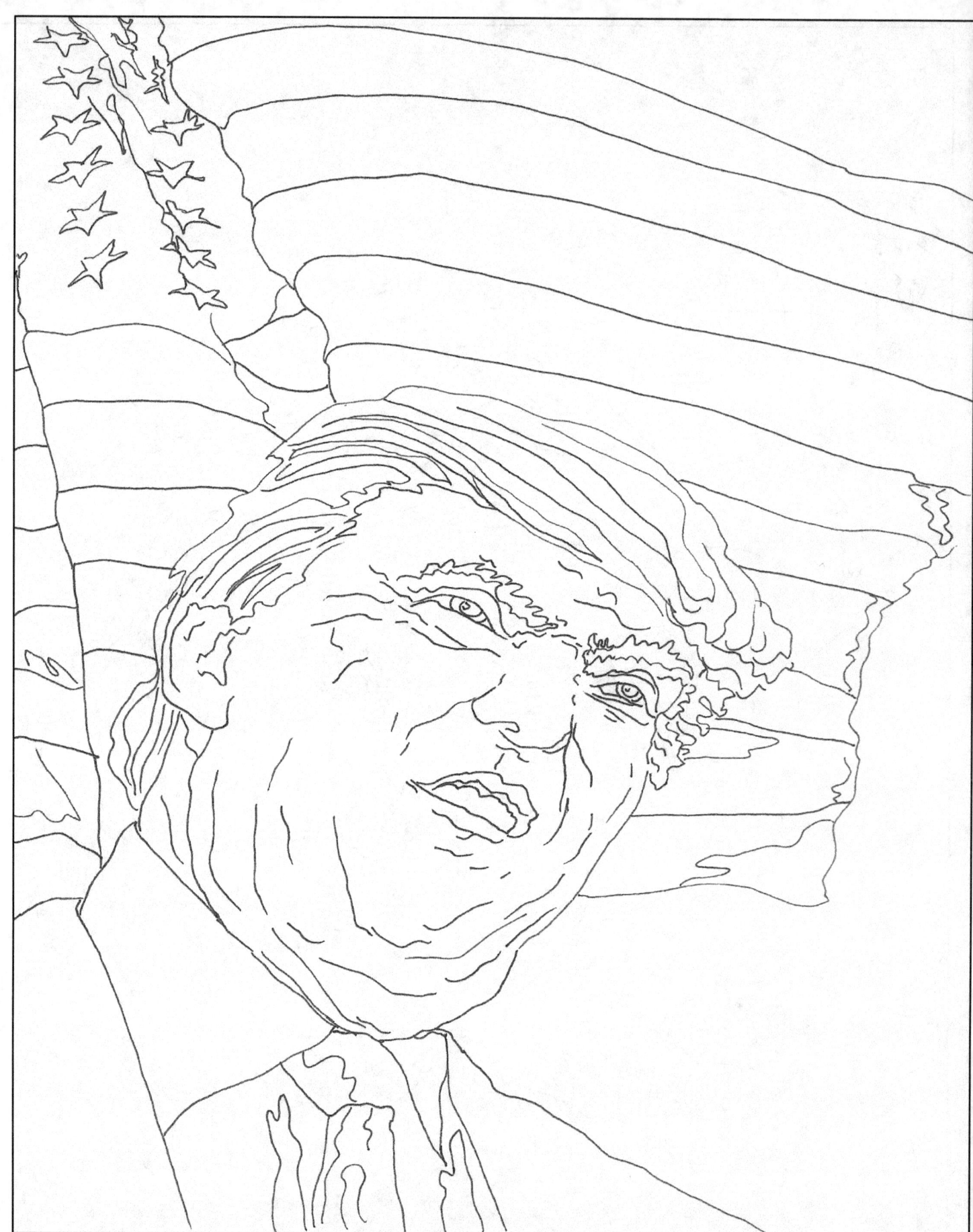

"Part of the beauty of me is that I am very rich."

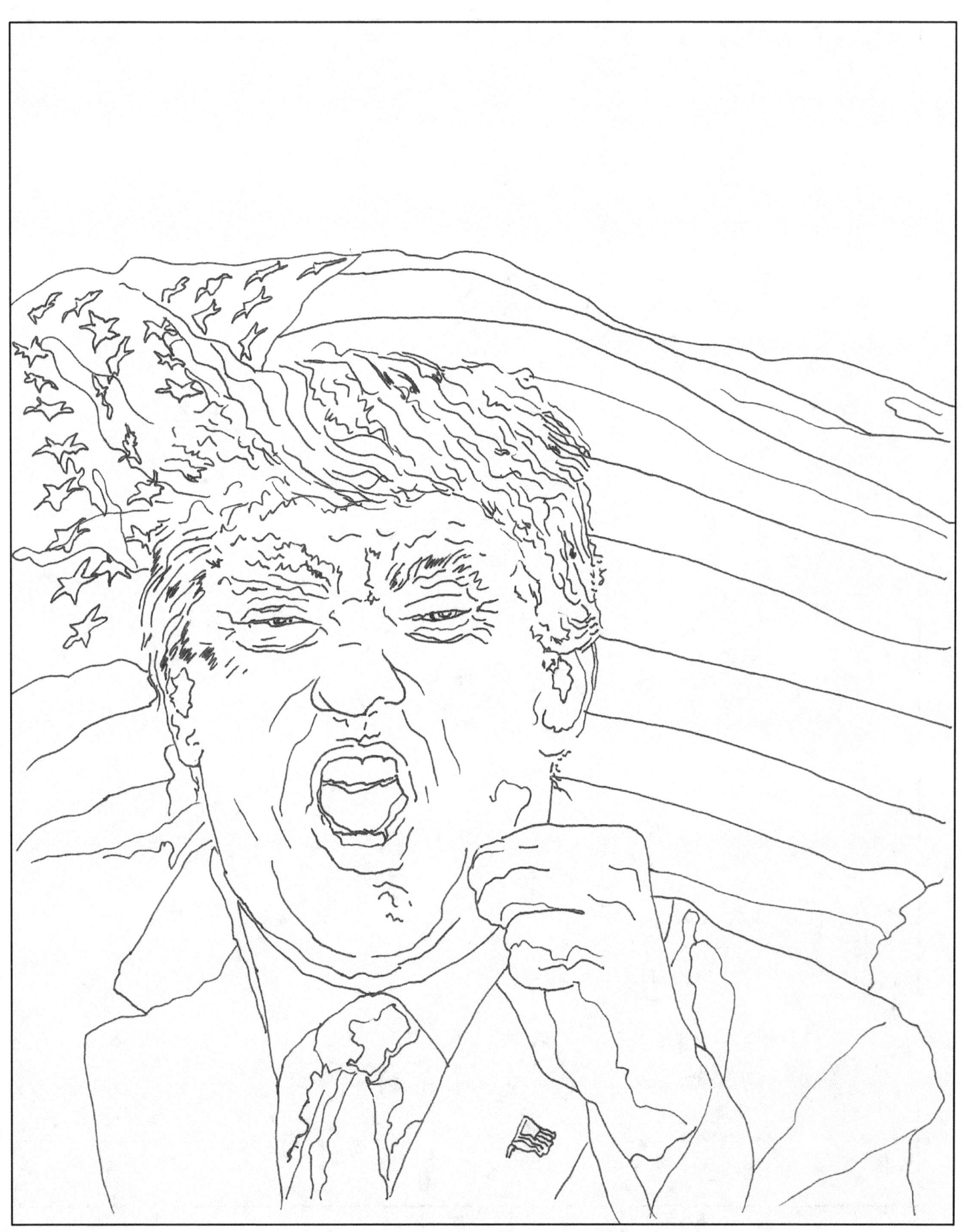

"I don't wear a 'rug'—it's mine. And I promise not to talk about
your massive plastic surgeries that didn't work."

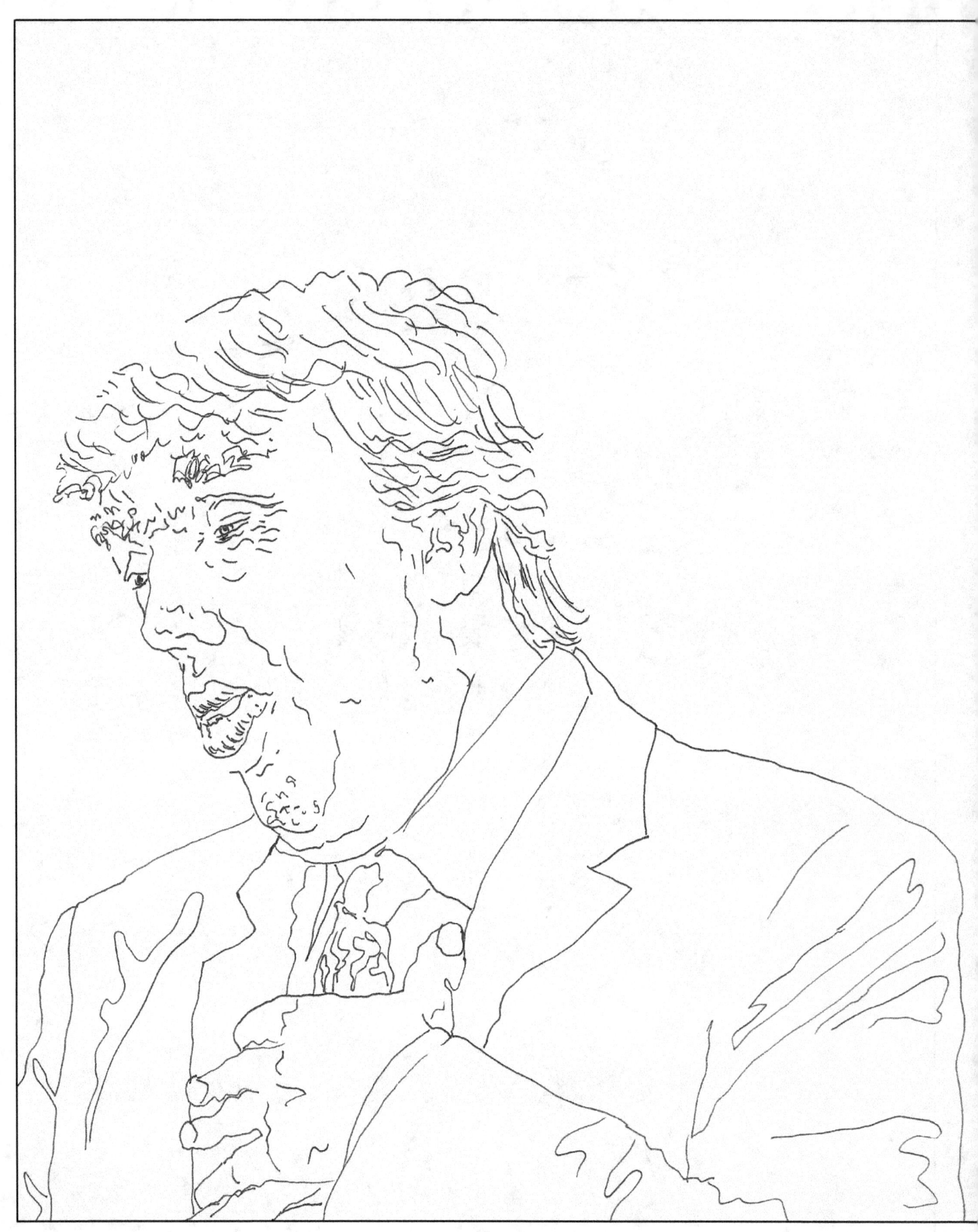

"I like people who weren't captured, . . . I don't like losers."

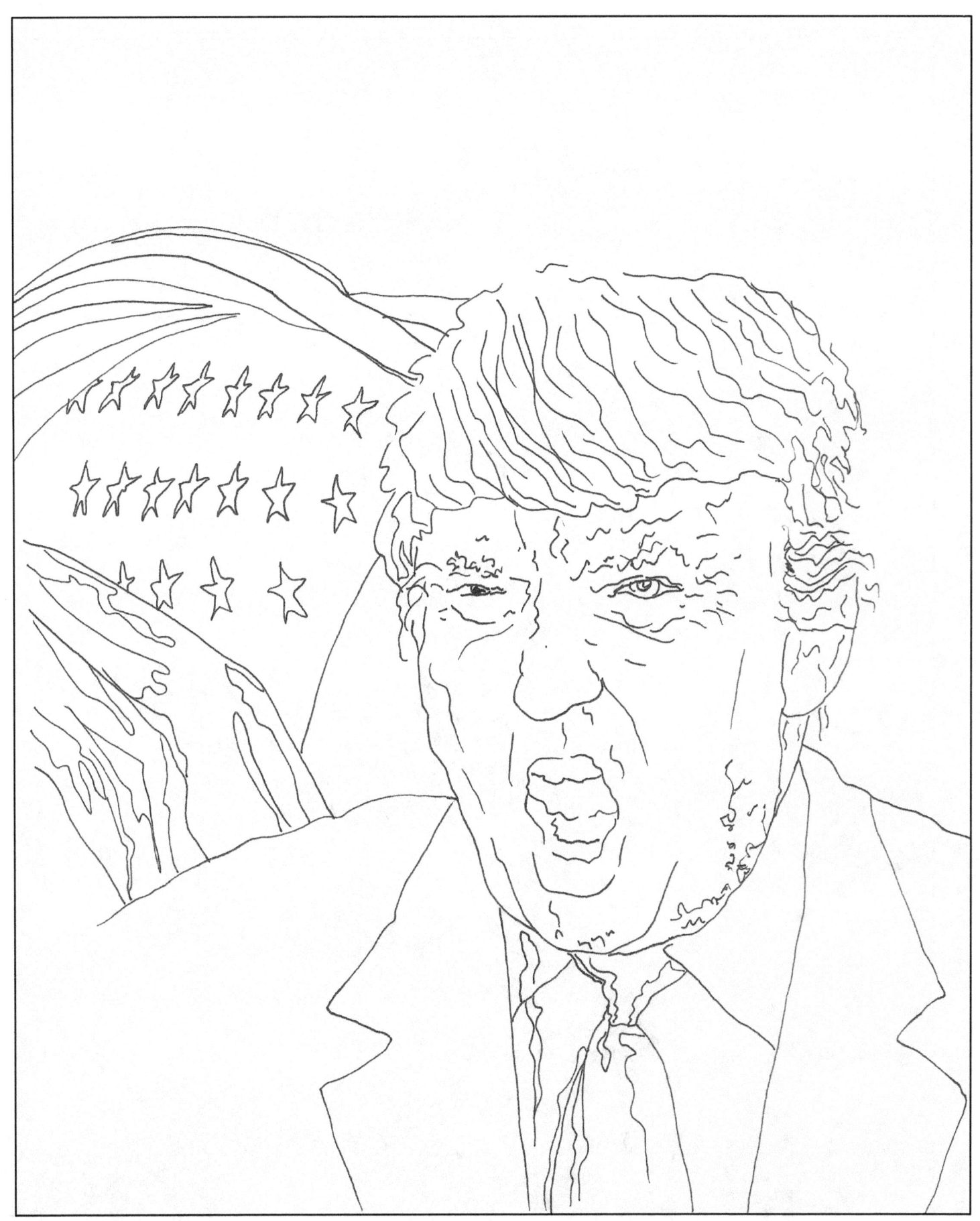

"If somebody screws you, screw them back in SPADES!"

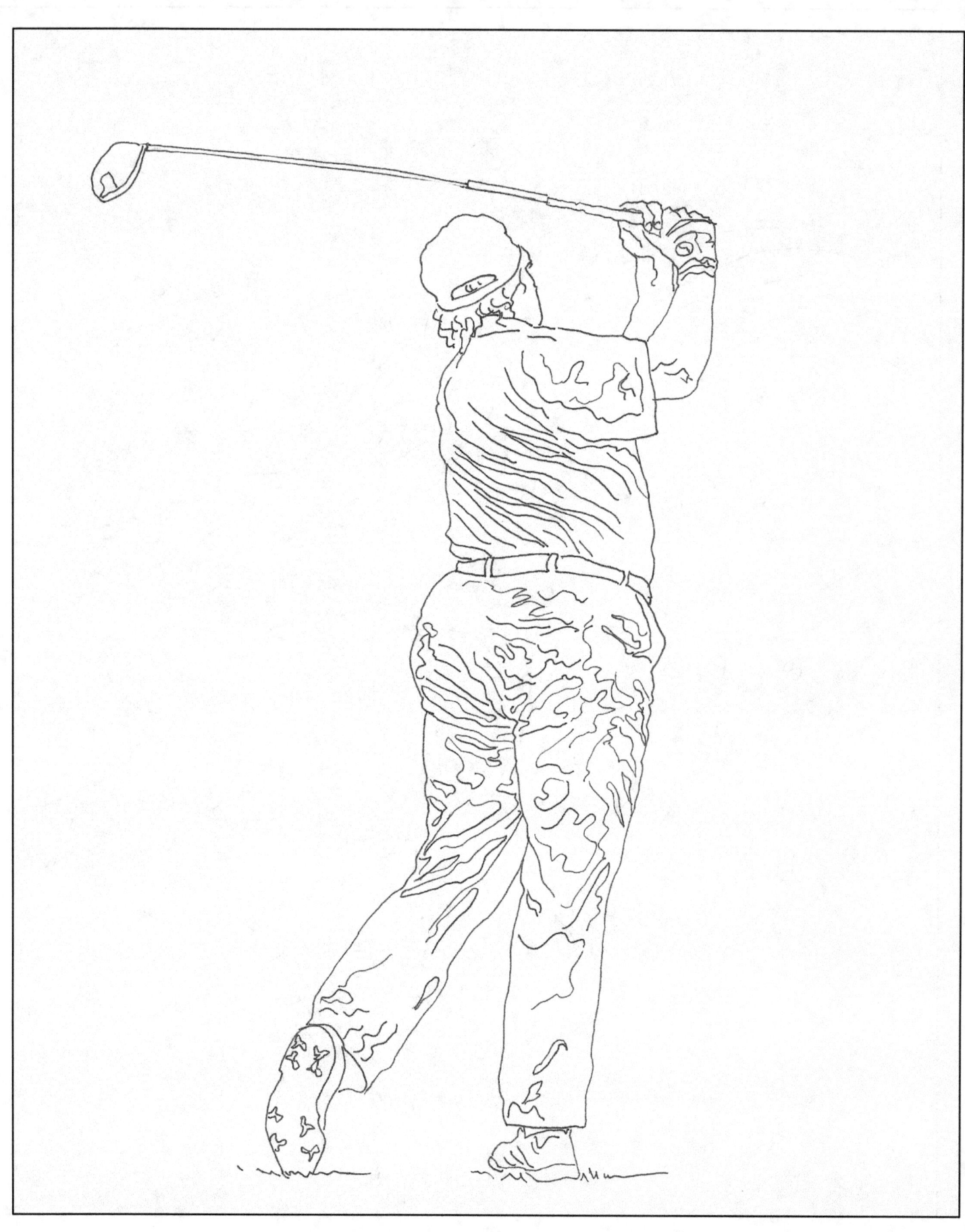

"The concept of global warming was created by and for the Chinese
in order to make U.S. manufacturing non-competitive."

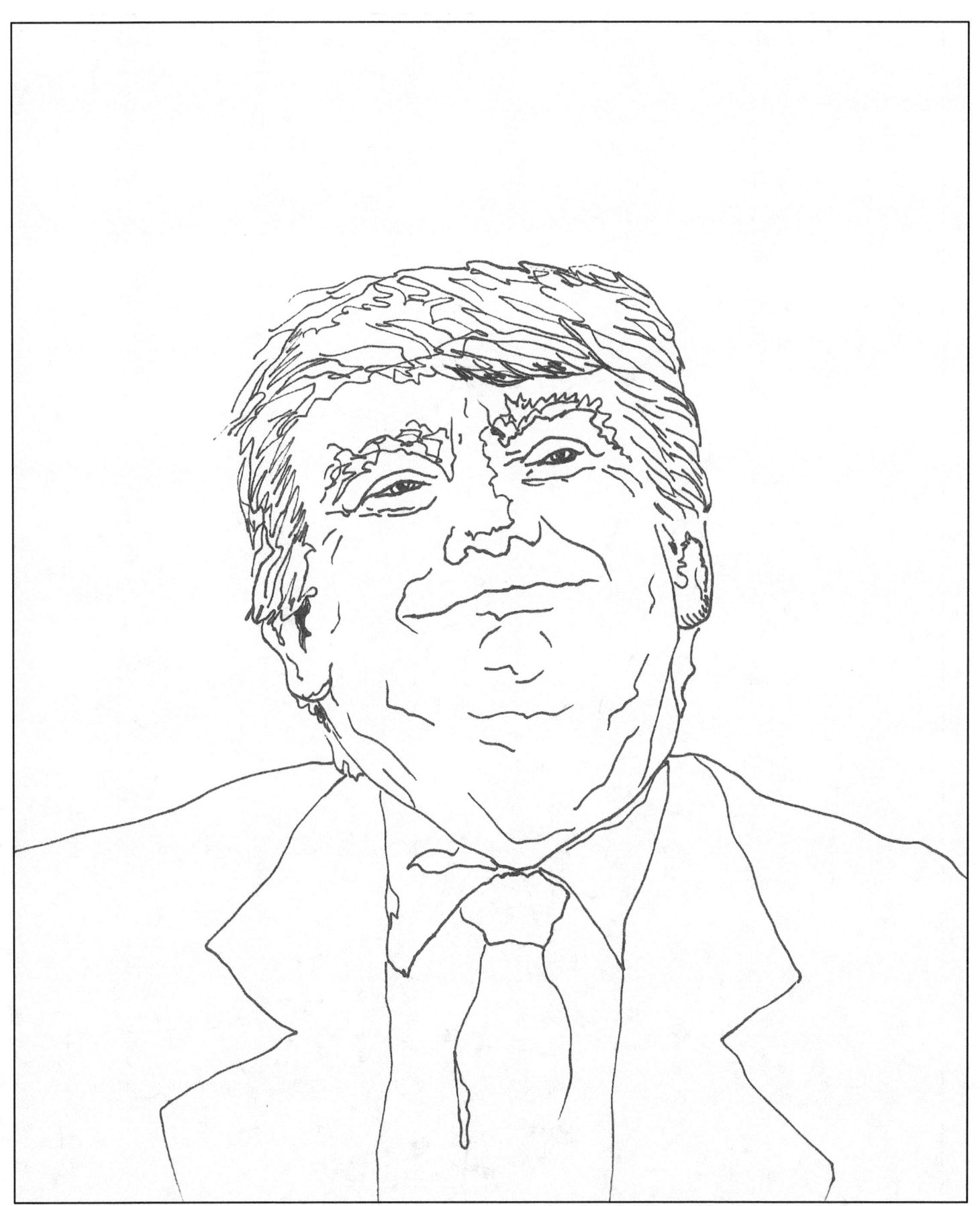

"I wouldn't mind a little bow. In Japan, they bow. I love it. Only thing I love about Japan."

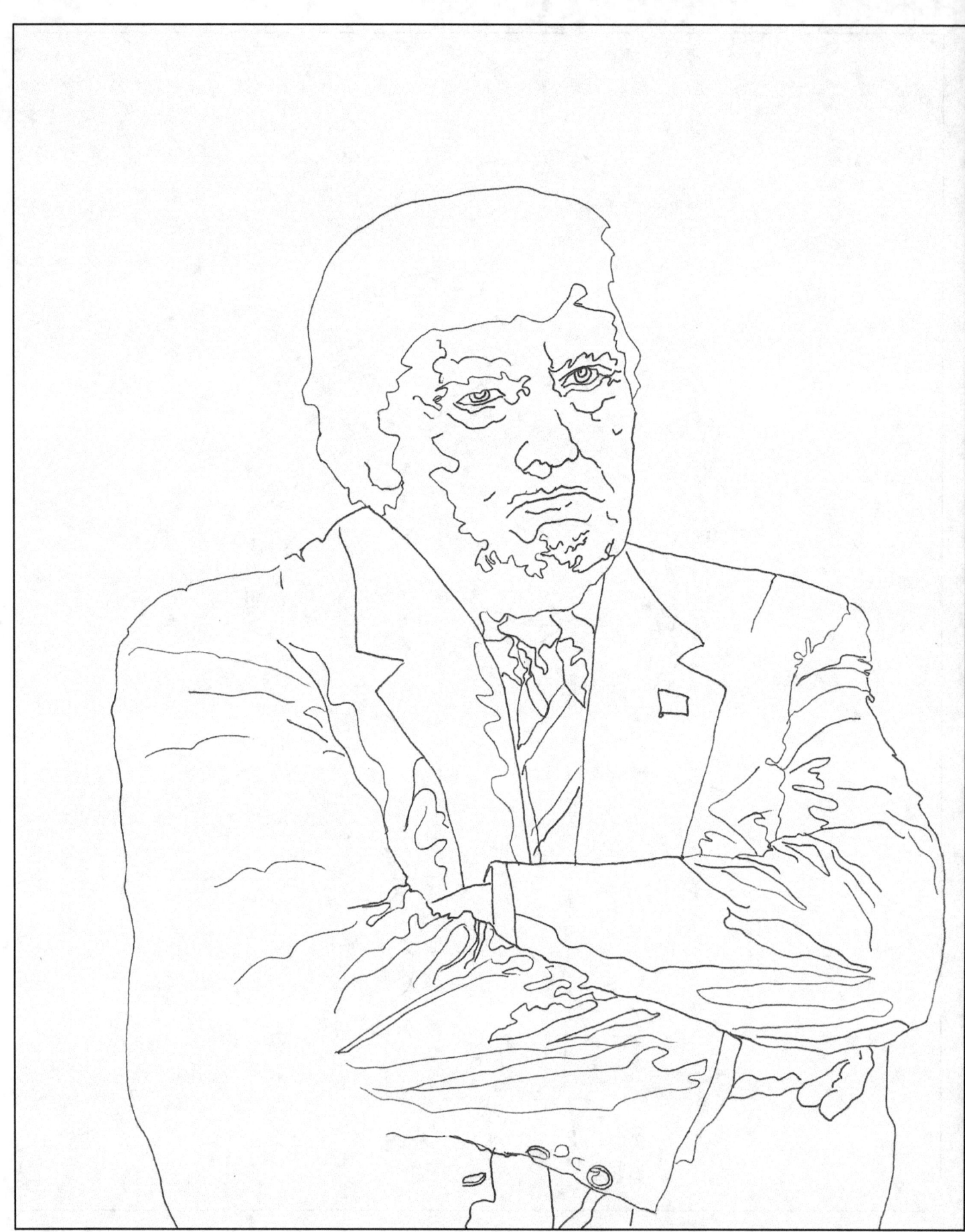

"When I think I'm right, nothing bothers me. Nothing gets too much under my skin."

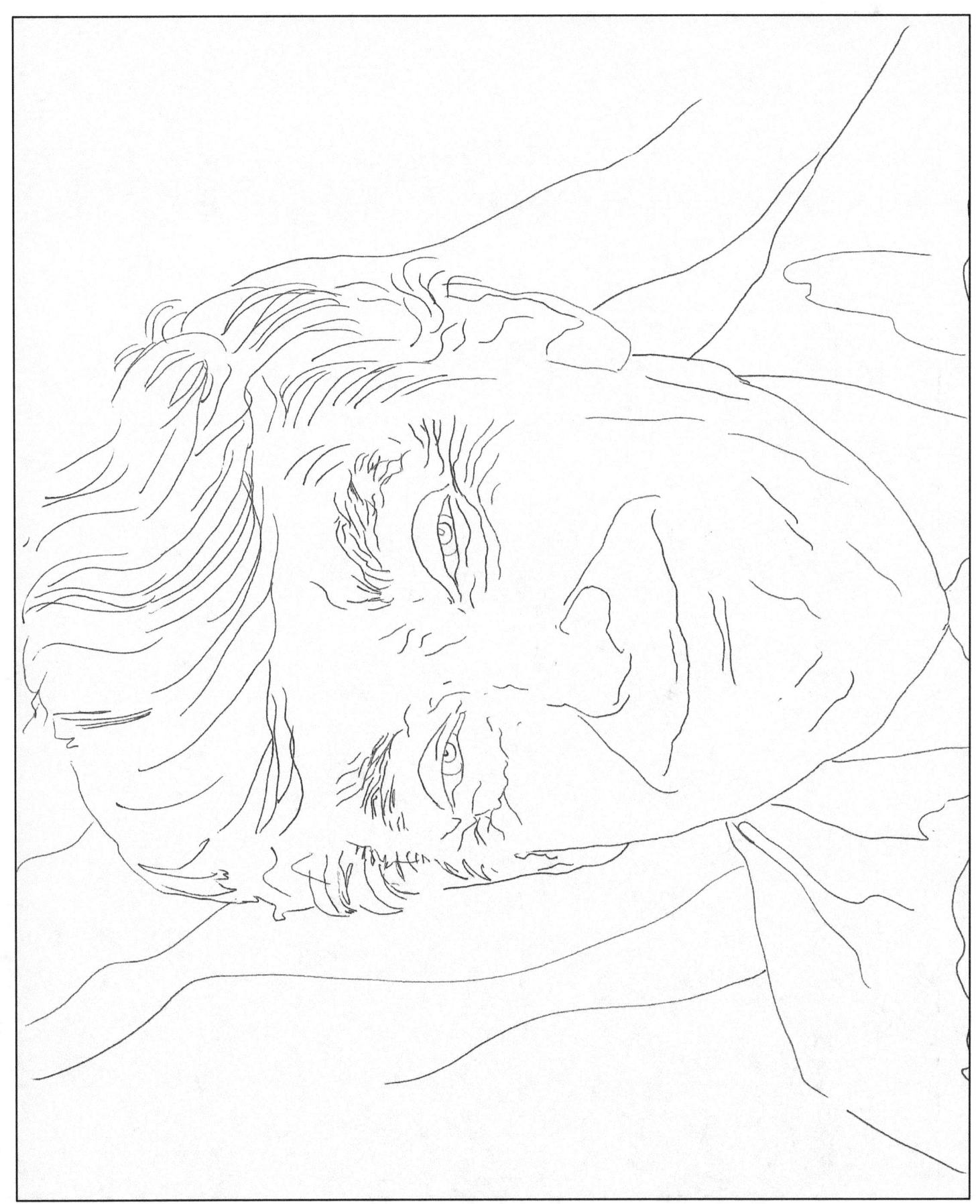

"I have a great relationship with the blacks."

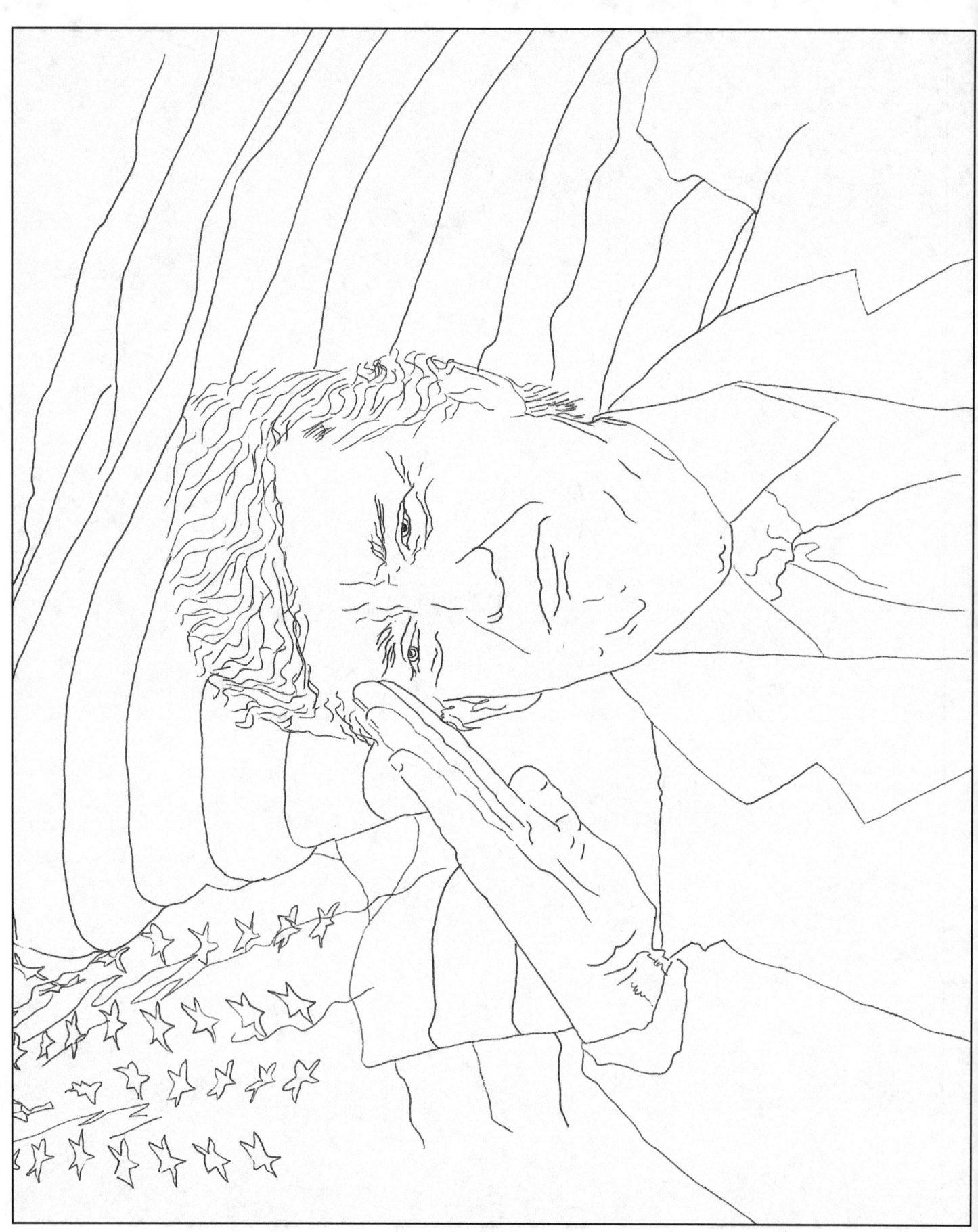

"I mean, you know, when you're asking me about who's running this, this this, that's not, that is not, I will be so good at the military, your head will spin."

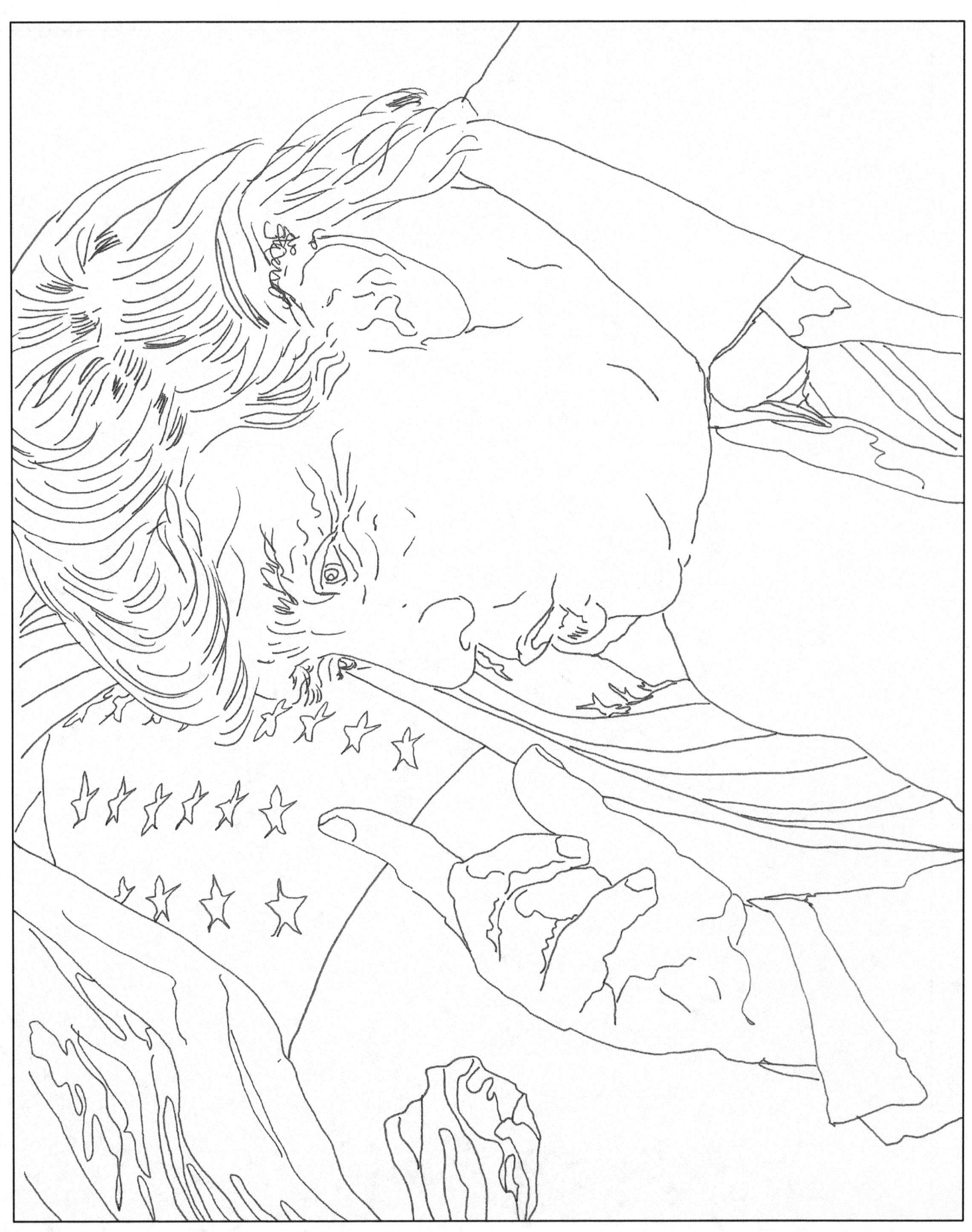

"Sorry losers and haters, but my I.Q. is one of the highest - and you all know it!
Please don't feel so stupid or insecure, it's not your fault."

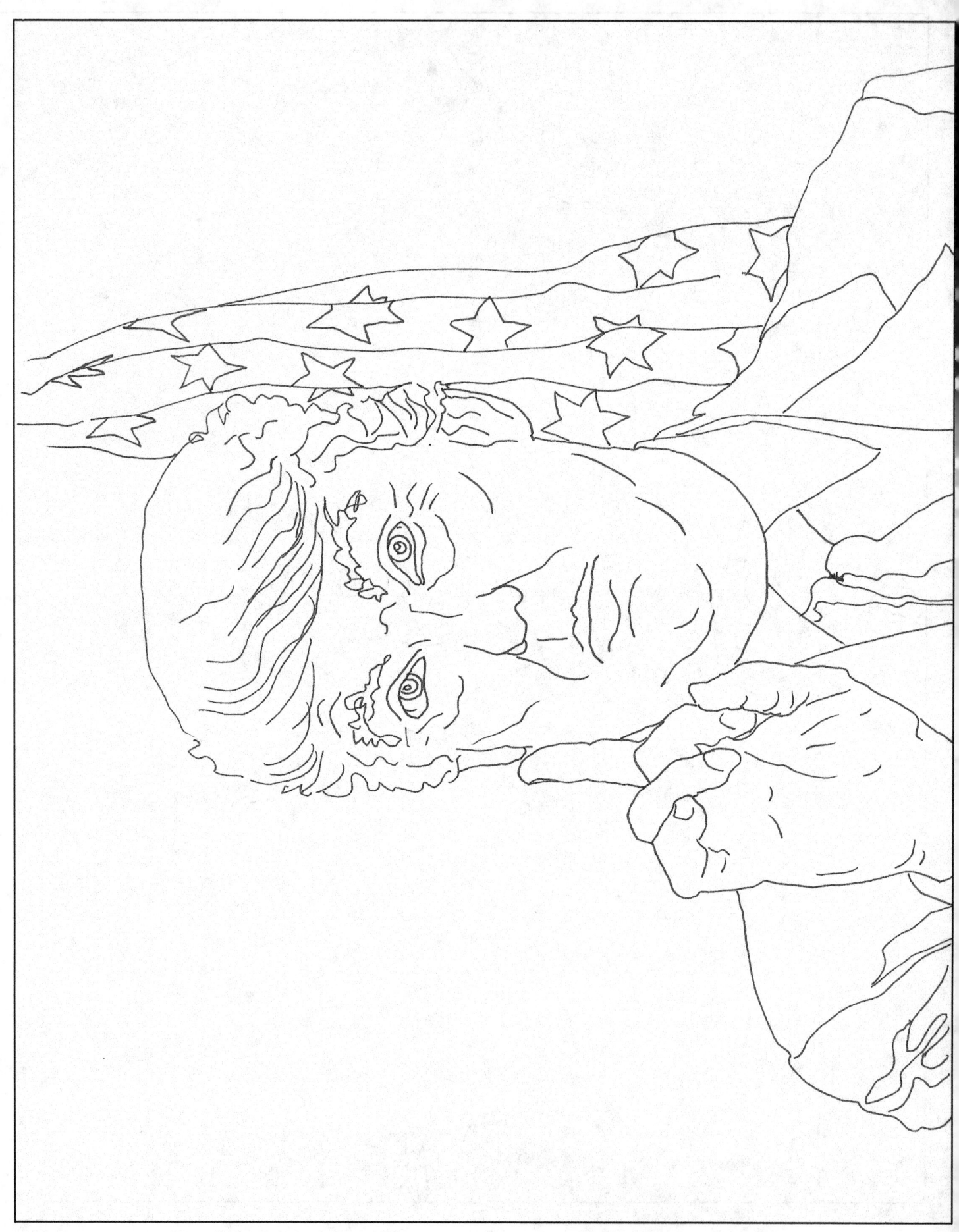

"The fake media tried to stop us from going to the White House.
But I'm president and they're not."

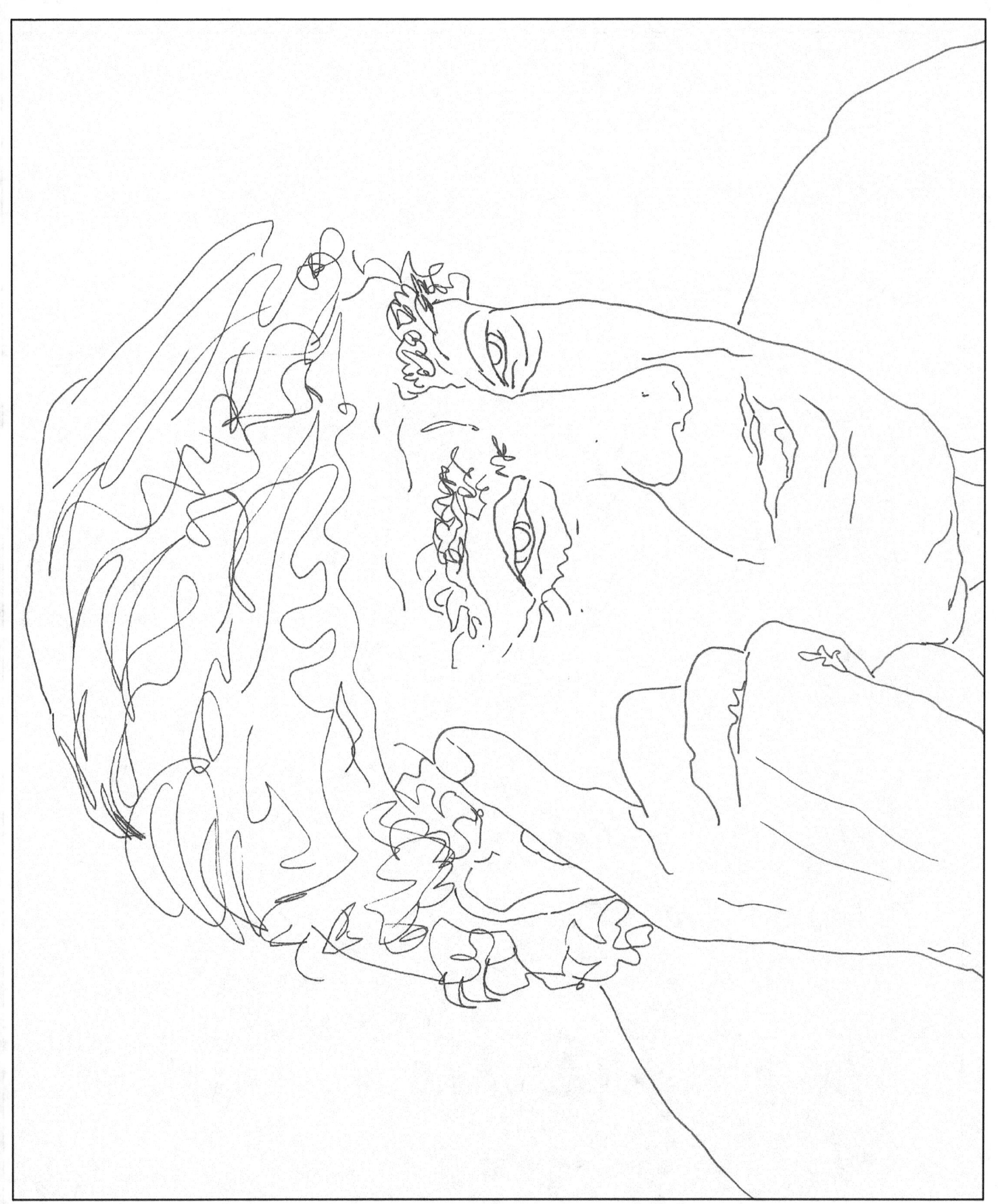

"There is something on that birth certificate — maybe religion,
maybe it says he's a Muslim, I don't know."

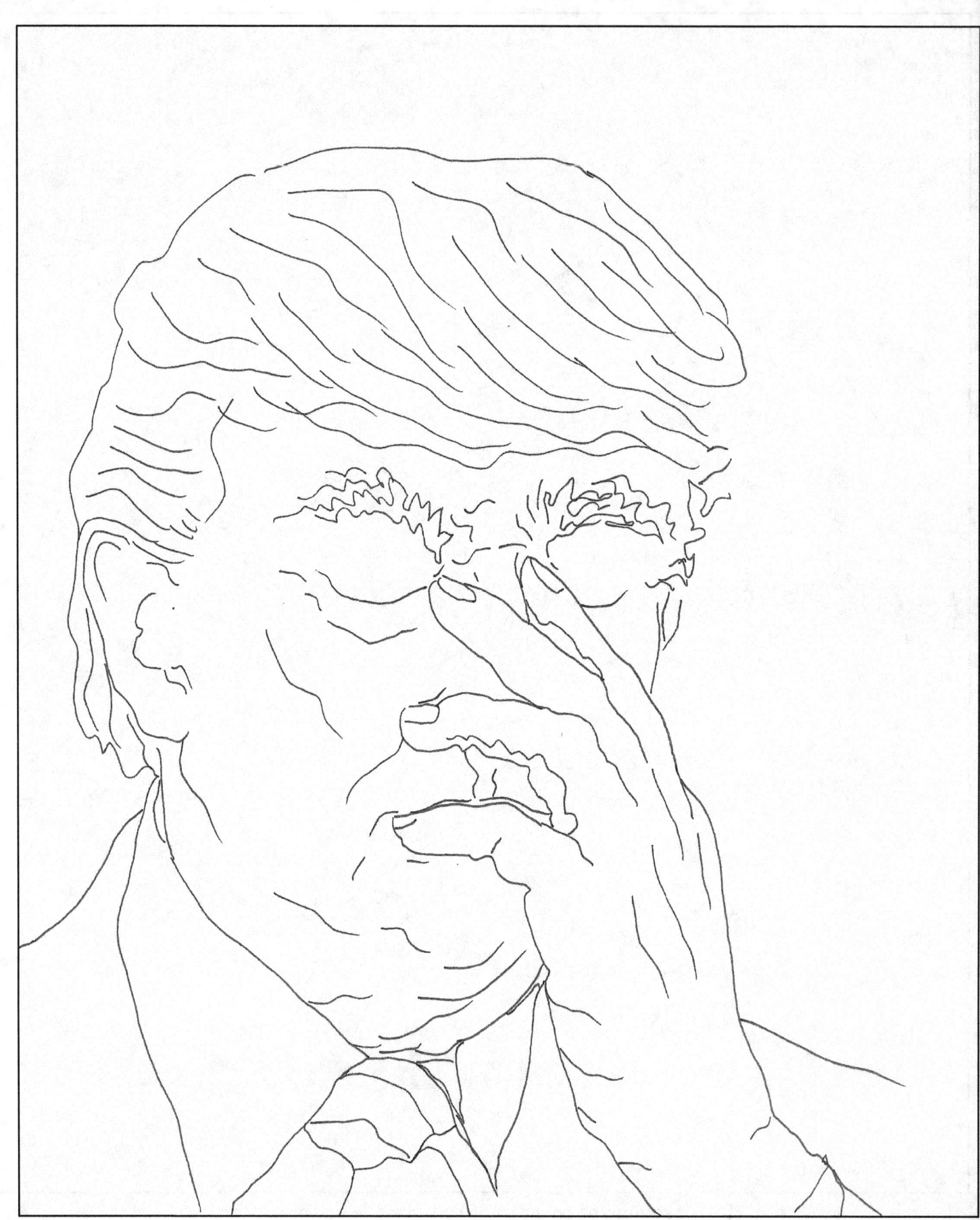

"Bing bing, bong bong, bing bing bing."

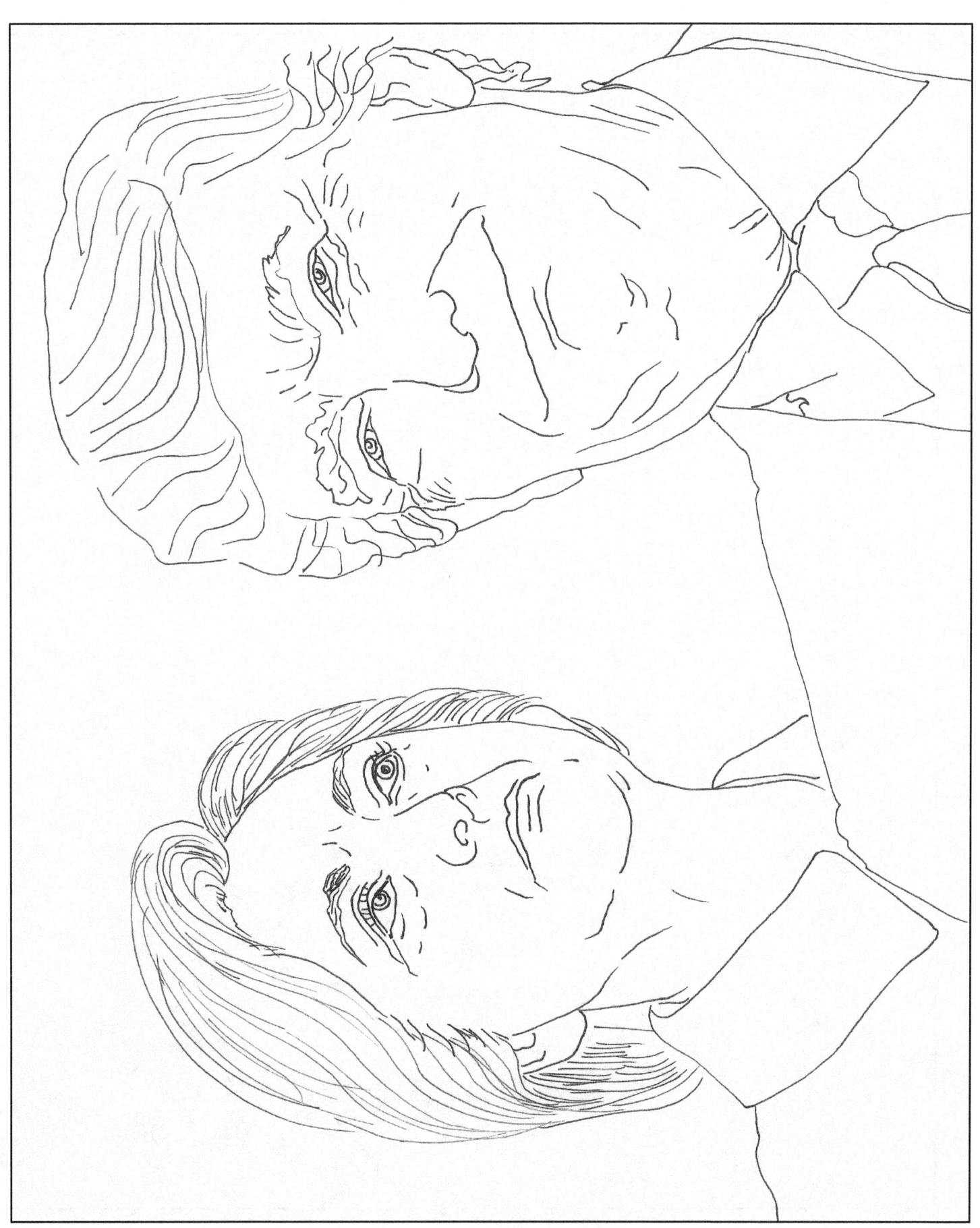

"Hillary's a very smart woman, very tough woman, that's fine.
She's also a very nice person. I think she's gonna go down
at a minimum as a great senator."

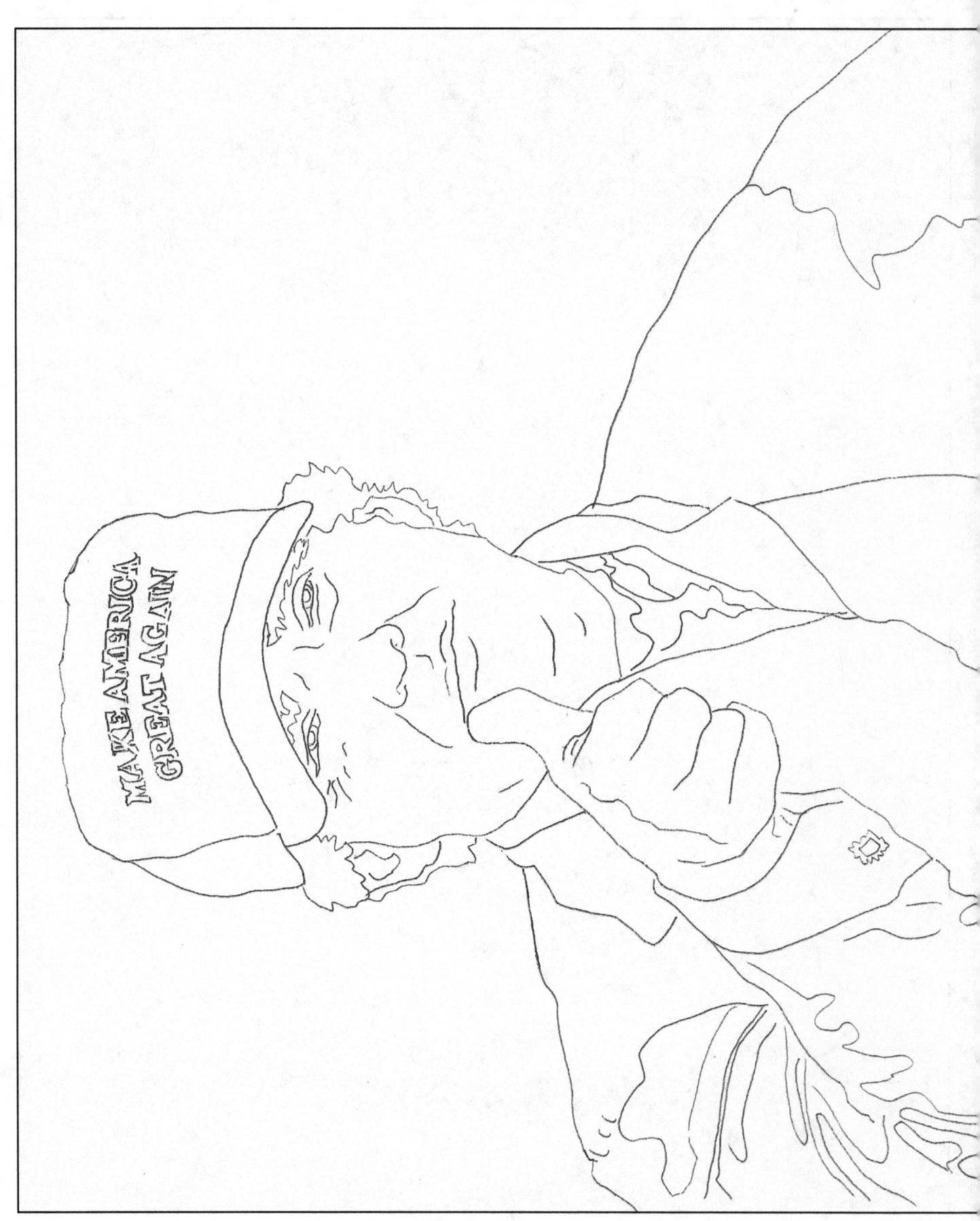

"How stupid are the people of Iowa? How stupid are the
people of the country to believe this crap?"

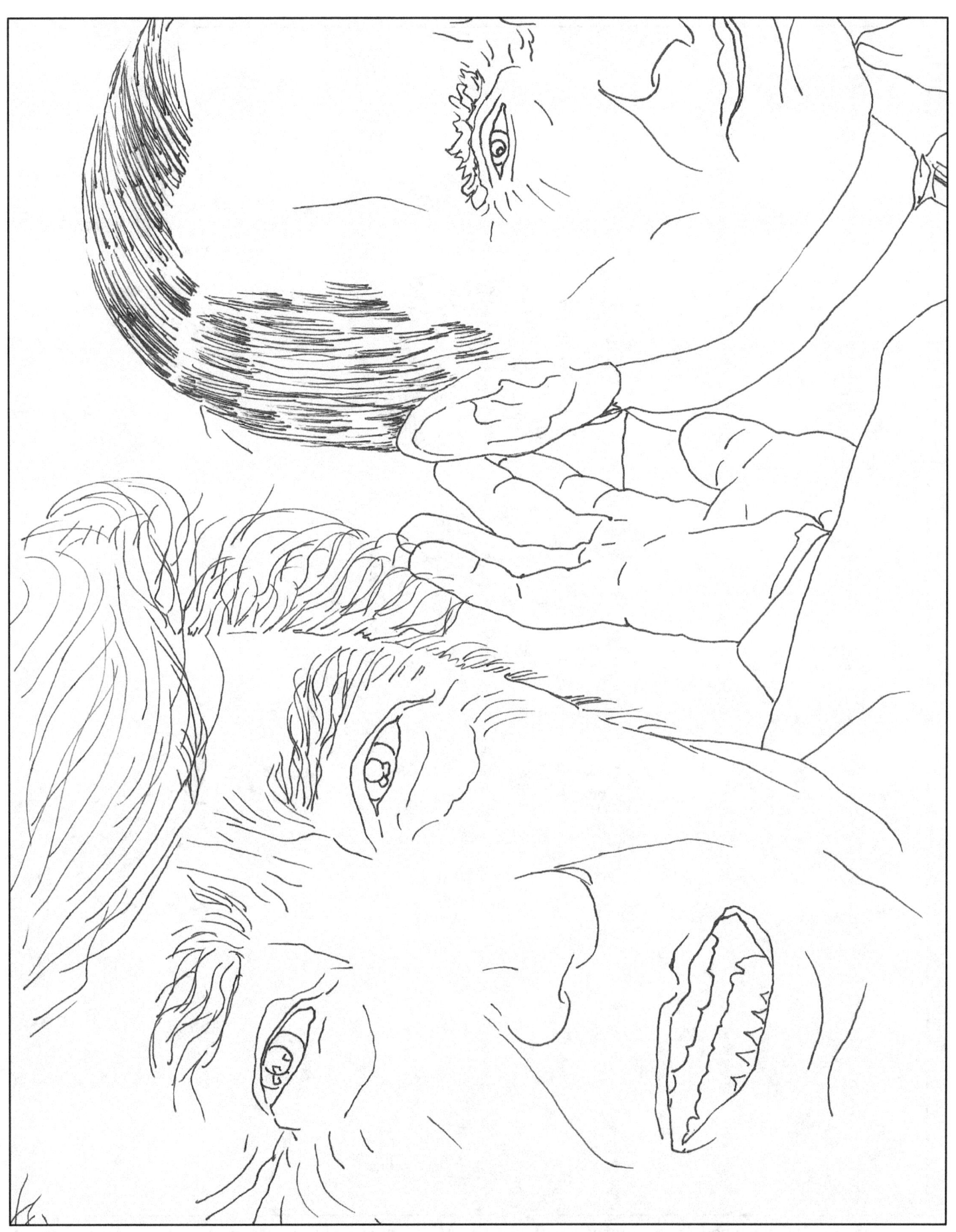

"Russia, if you're listening..."

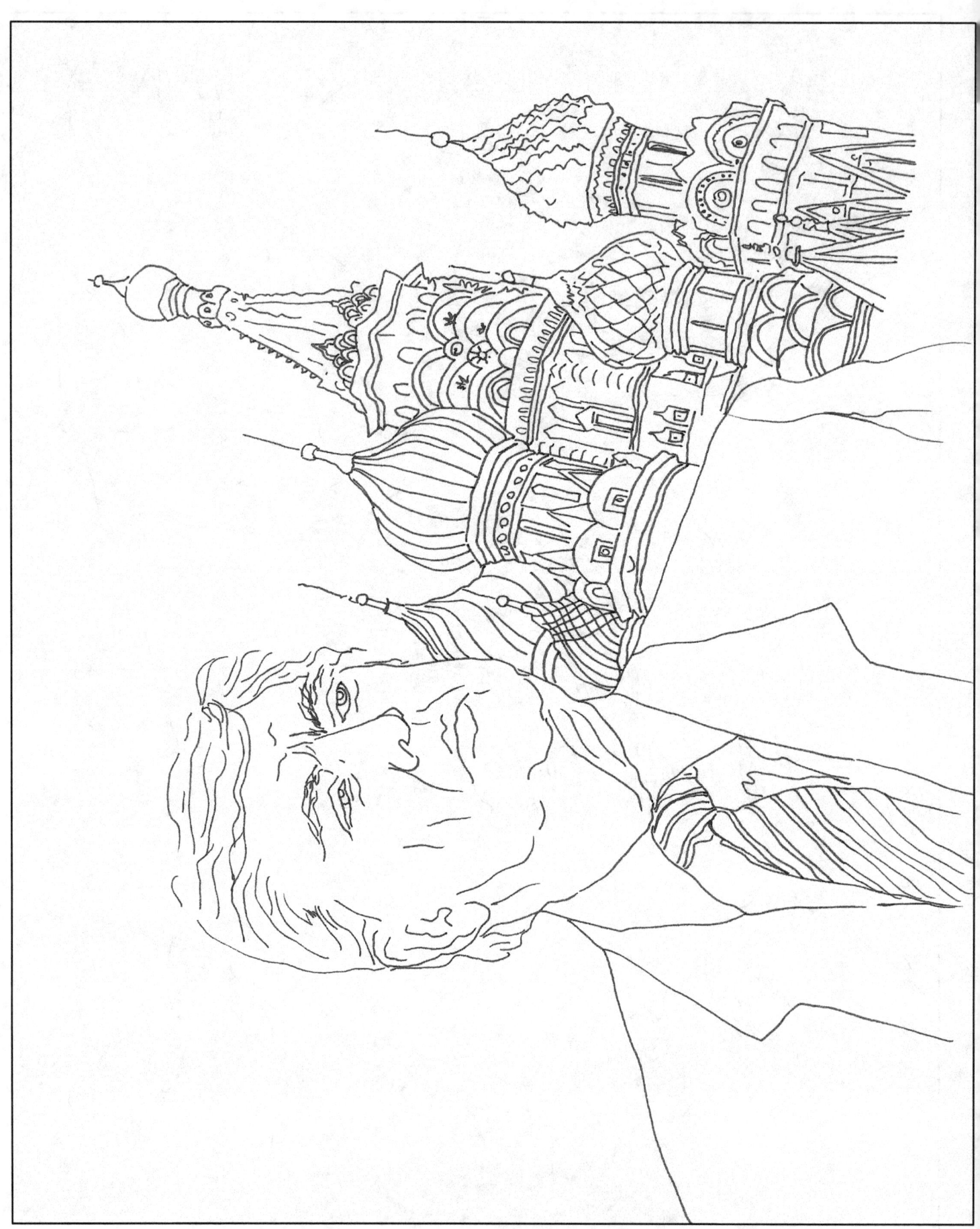

"I was in Moscow a couple of months ago, I own the Miss Universe Pageant and they treated me so great. Putin even sent me a present, a beautiful present."

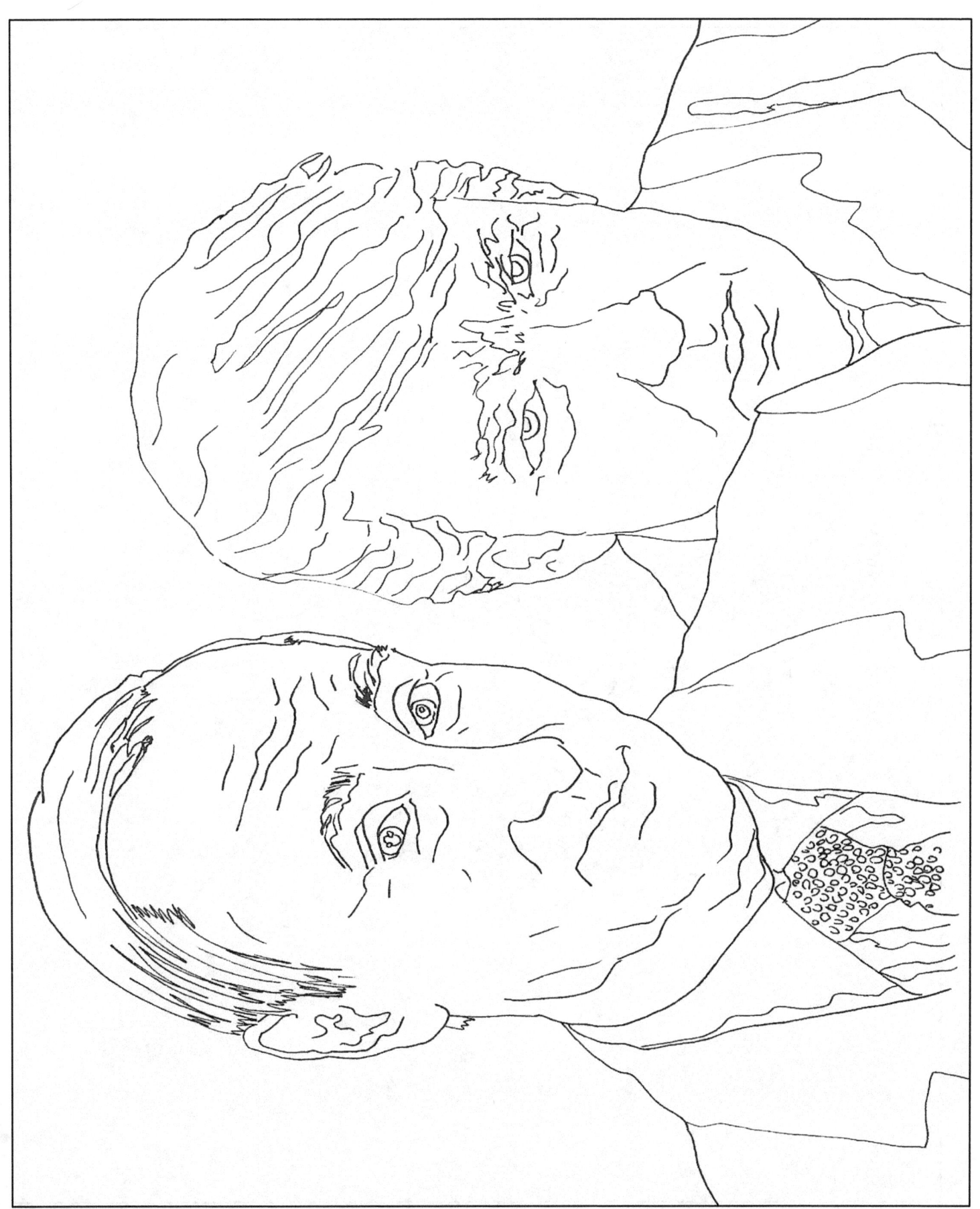

"He's running his country, and at least he's a leader.
Unlike what we have in this country."

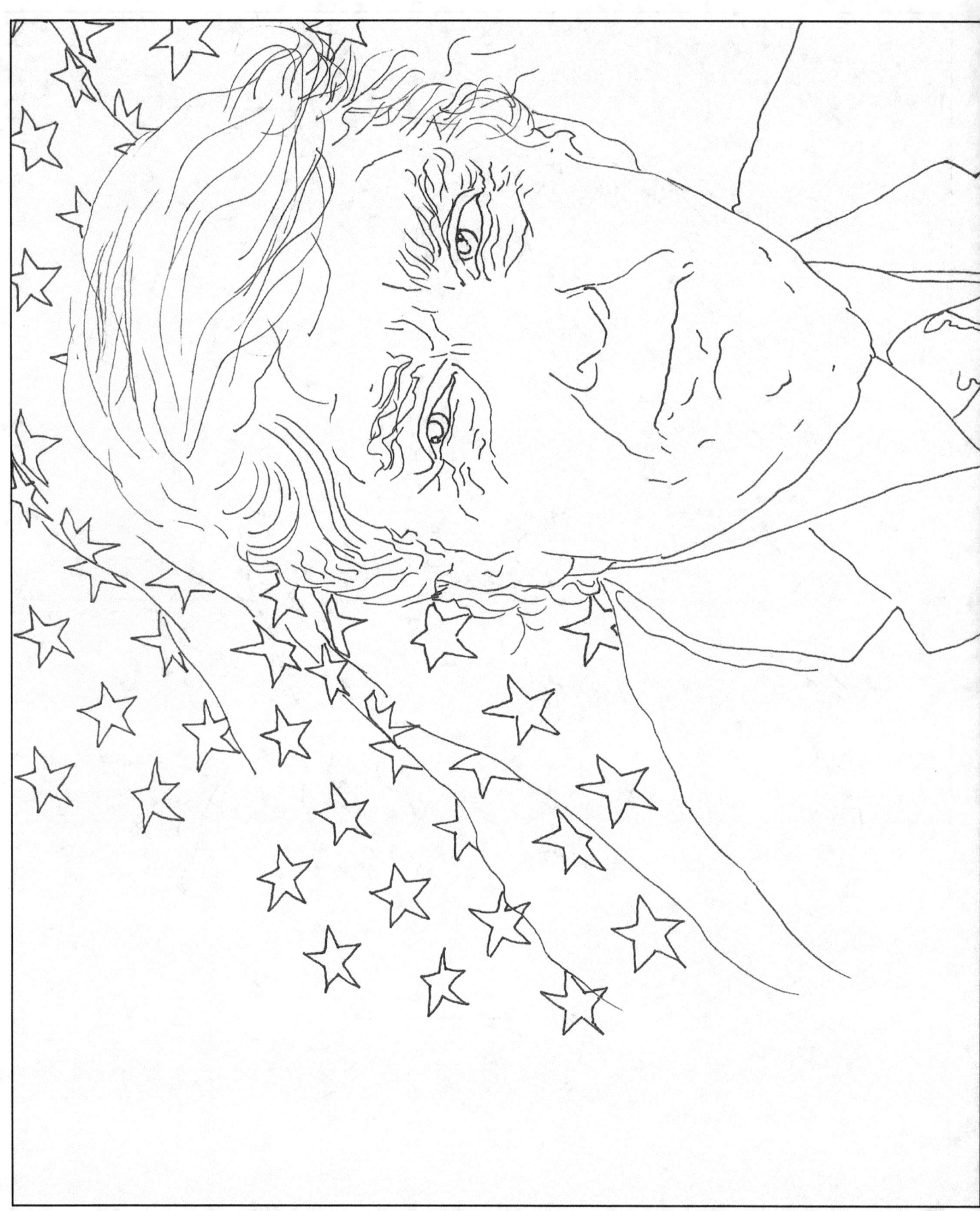

"She does have a very nice figure. I've said that if Ivanka
weren't my daughter, perhaps I'd be dating her."

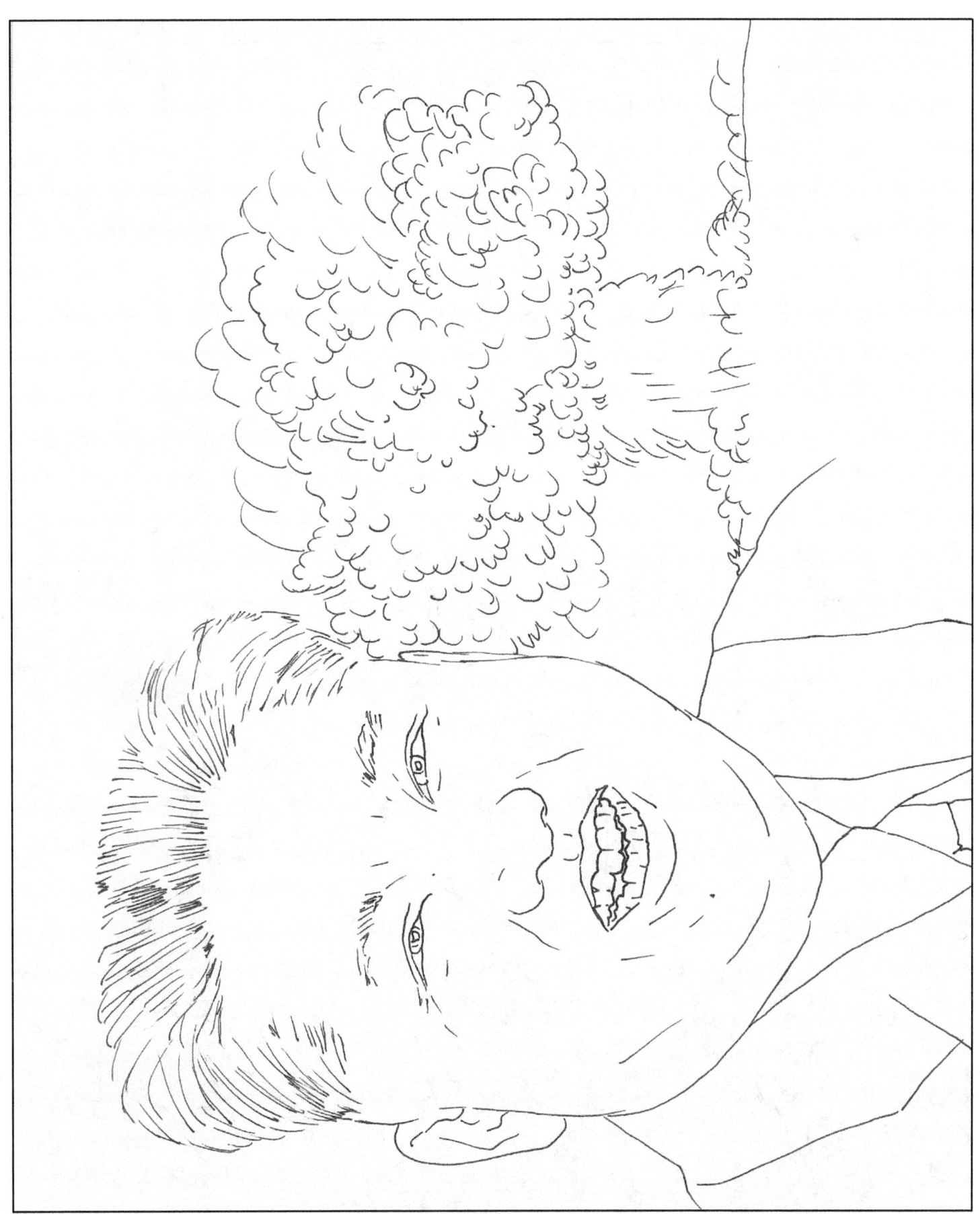

"So obviously, he's a pretty smart cookie."

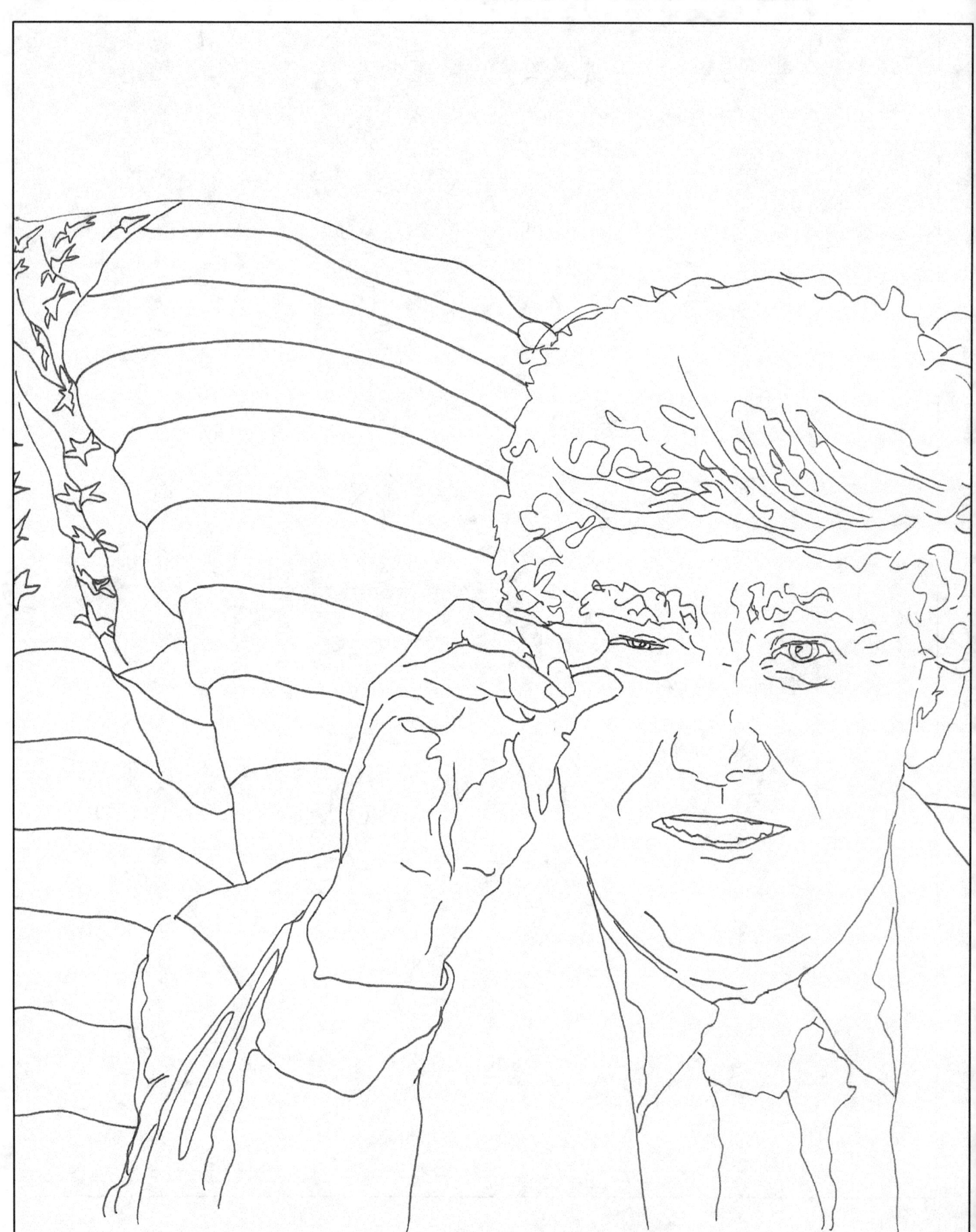

"Do you mind if I sit back a little? Because your breath is very bad
—it really is." —

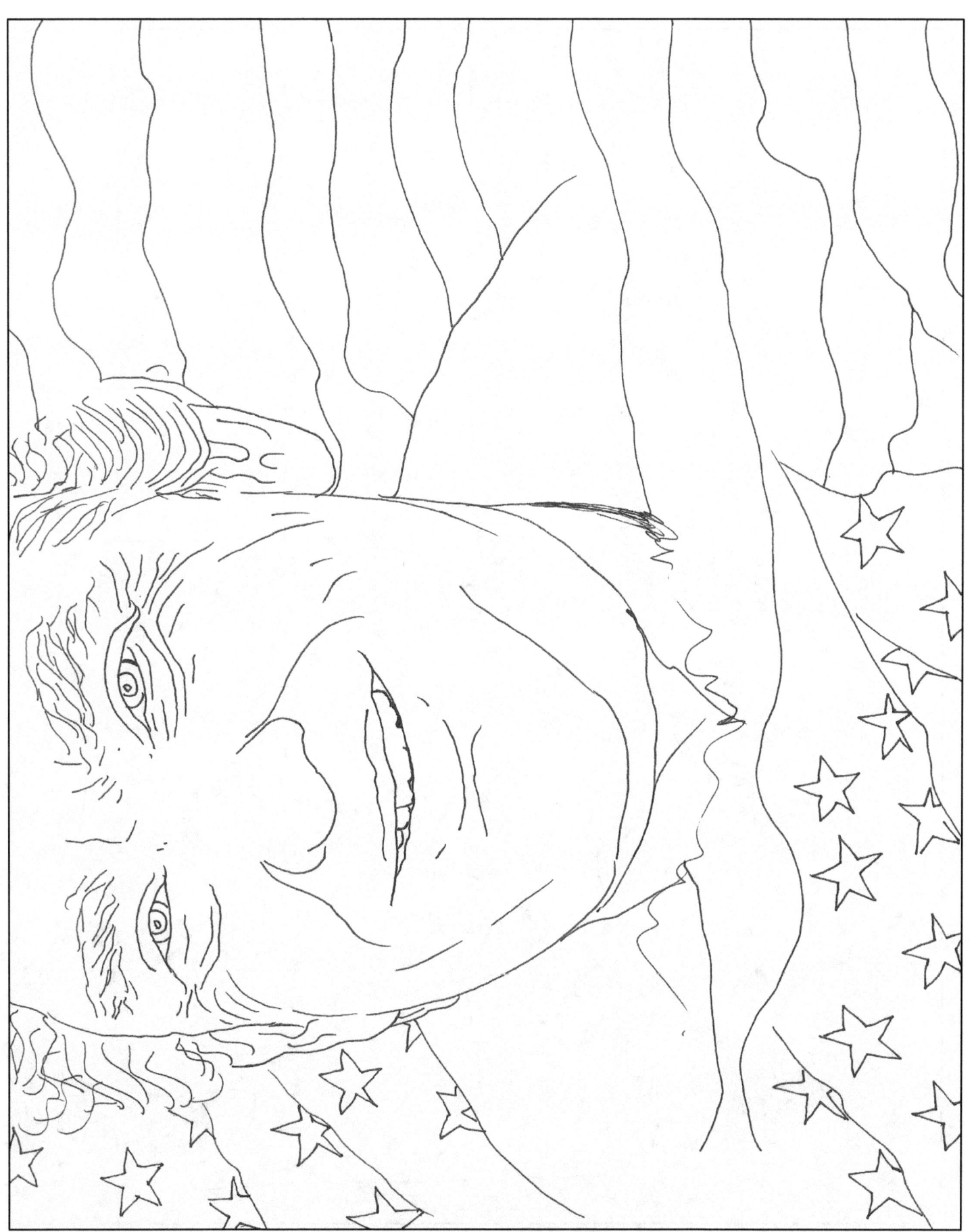

"In the second grade I actually gave a teacher a black eye —
I punched my music teacher because I didn't think he knew
anything about music and I almost got expelled."

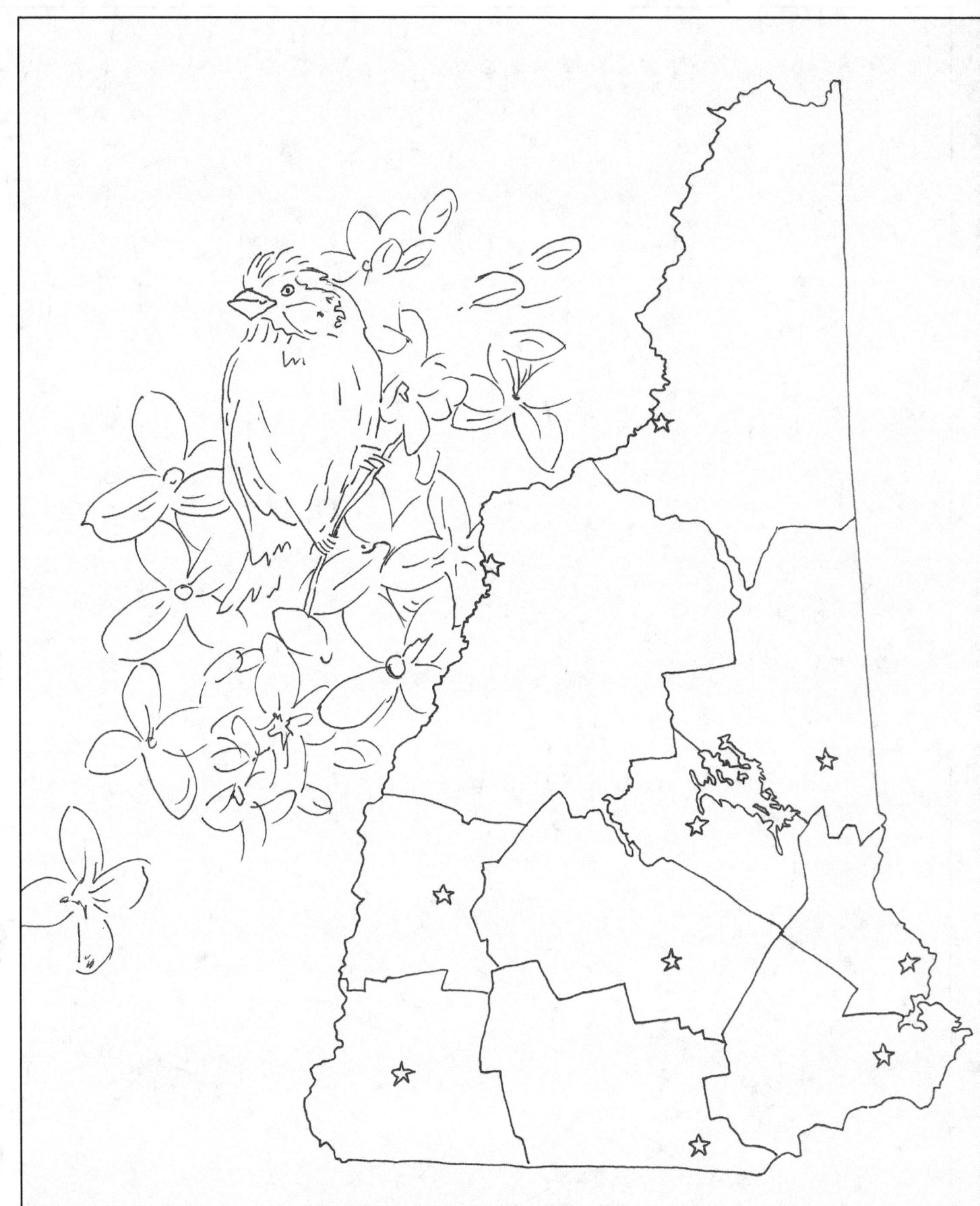

"I won New Hampshire because New Hampshire
is a drug-infested den."

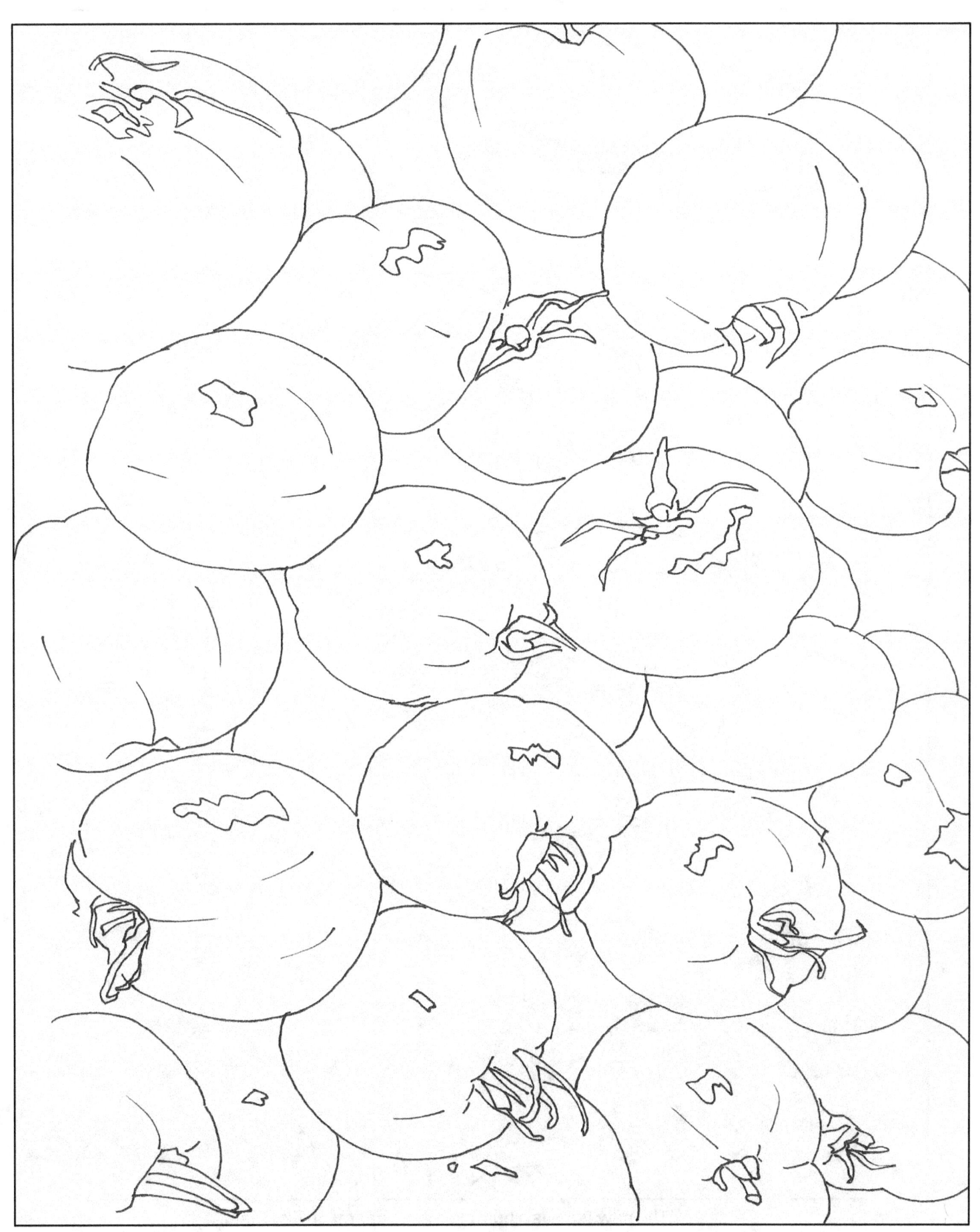

"If you see somebody getting ready to throw a tomato,
knock the crap out of them."

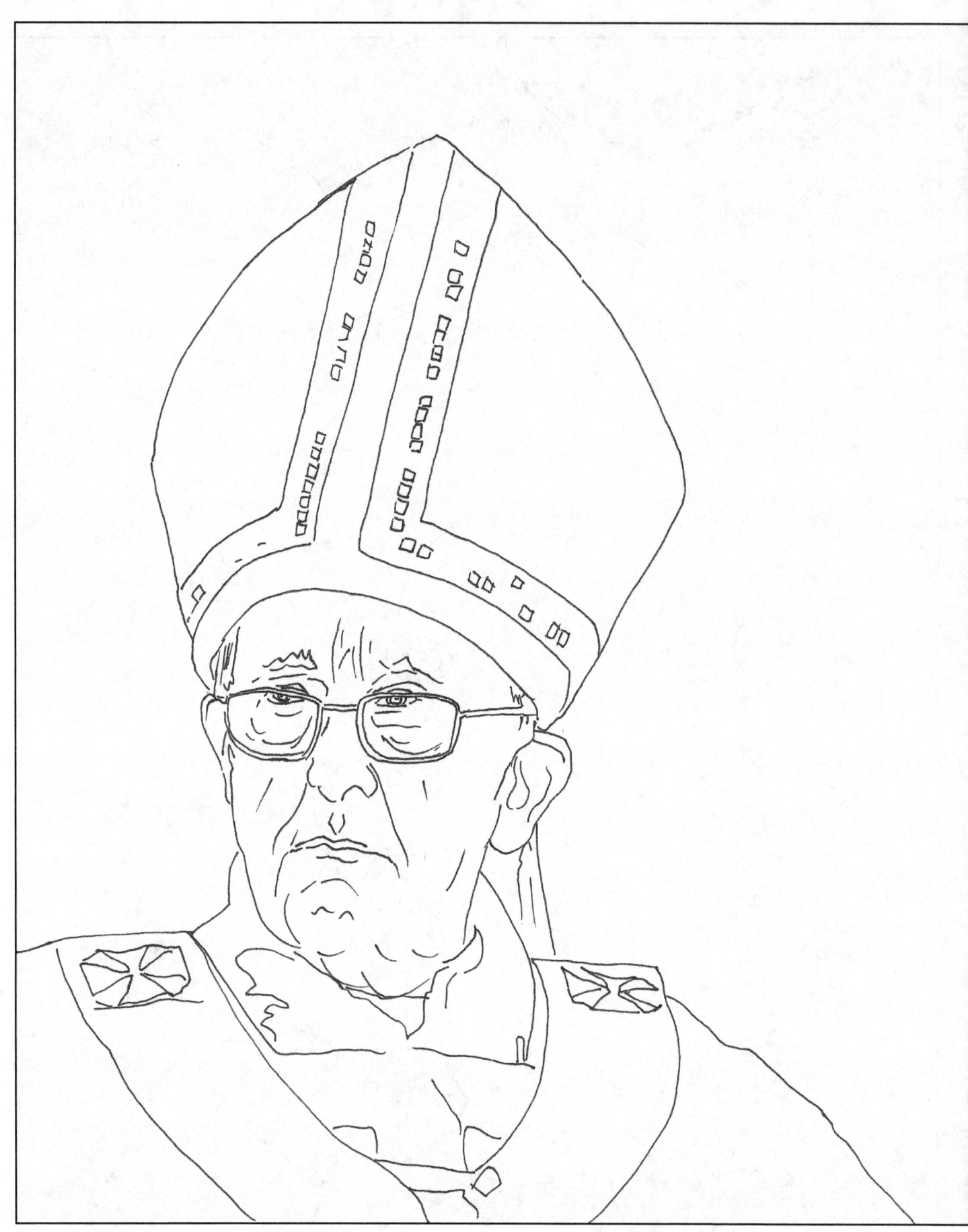

"The new Pope is a humble man, very much like me,
which probably explains why I like him so much."

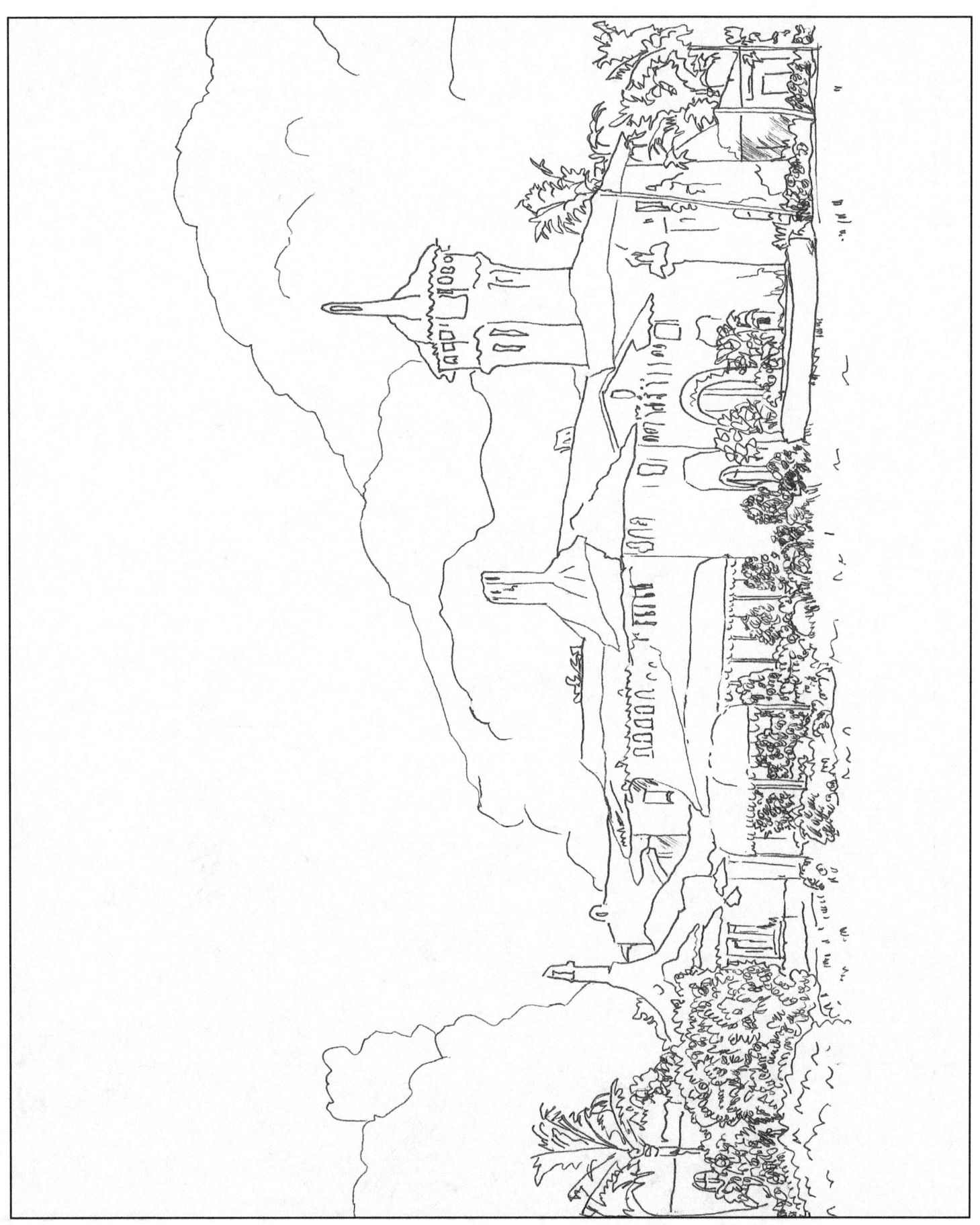

"Writing my inaugural address at the
Winter White House, Mar-a-Lago."

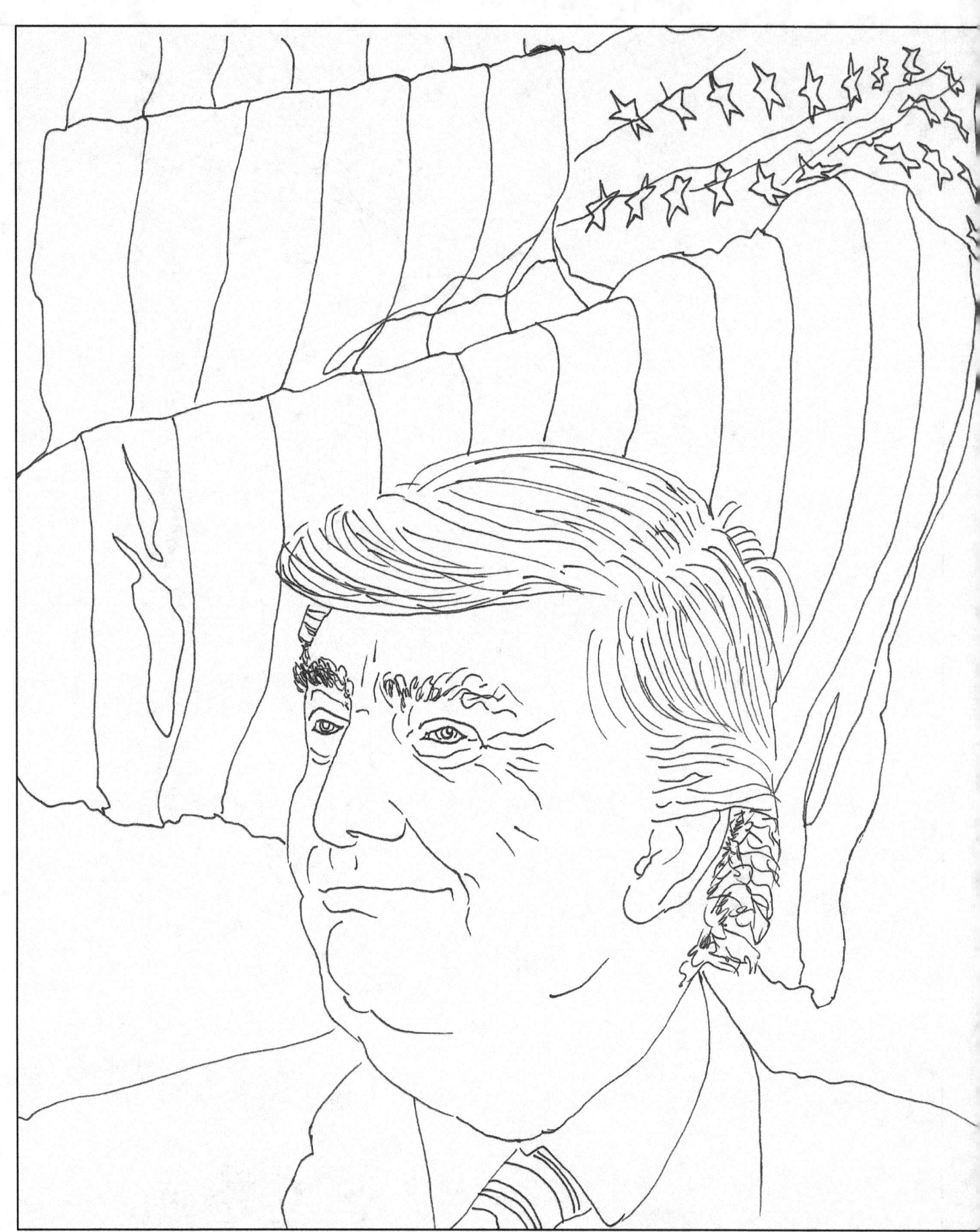

"It would take an hour and a half to learn everything there is
to learn about missiles. ... I think I know most of it anyway."

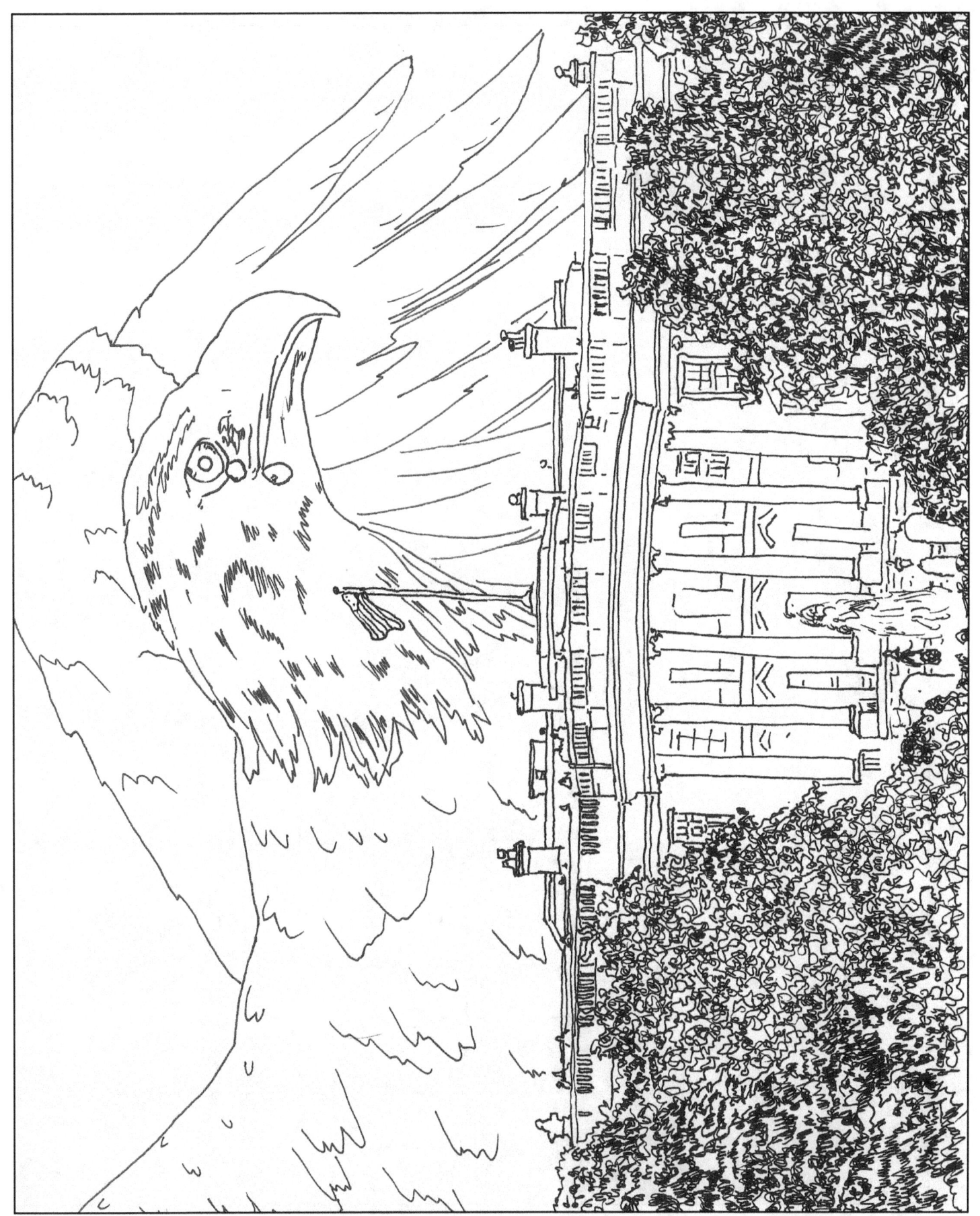

"That White House is a real dump."

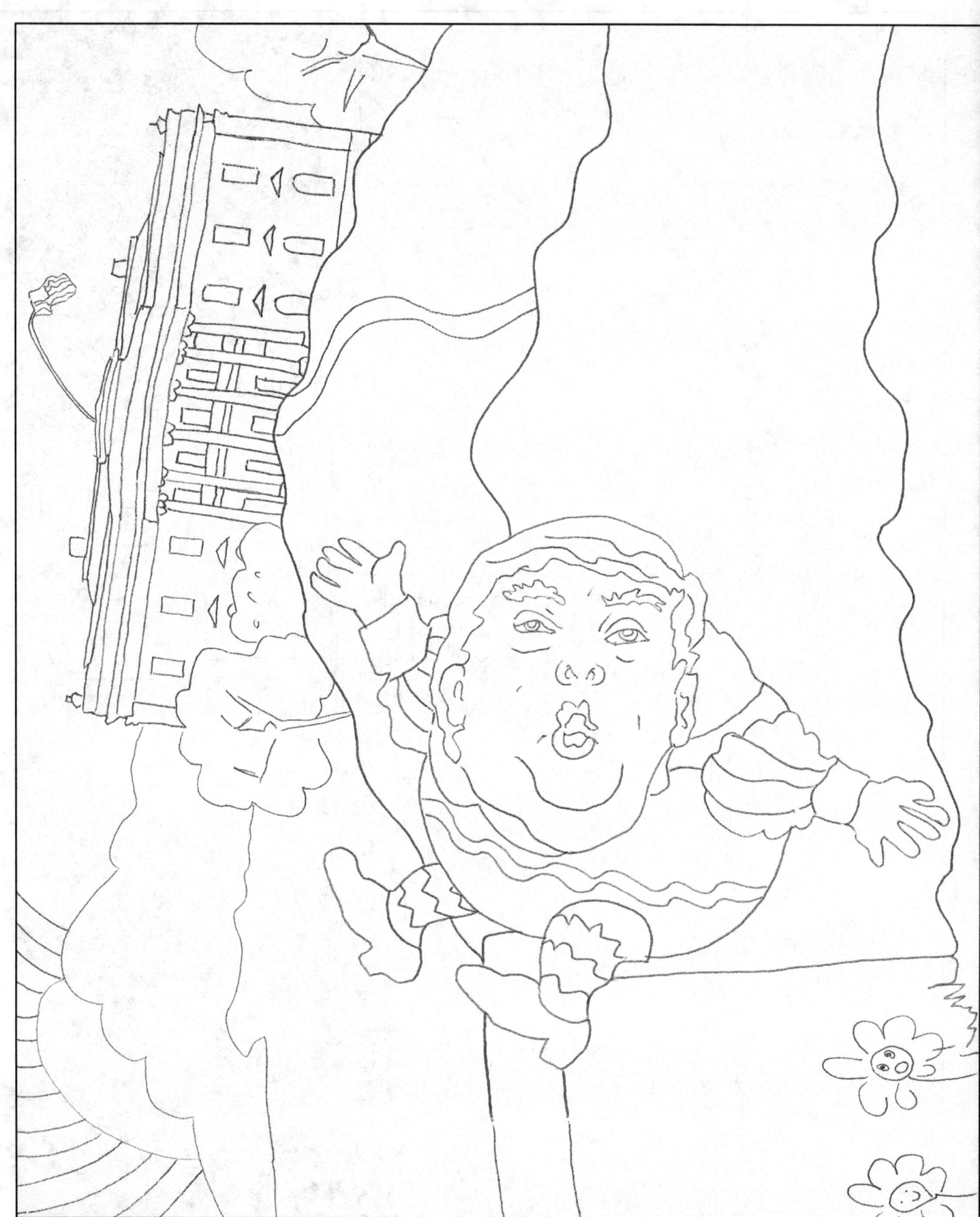

"We're going to win bigly."

1. Happy Cinco de Mayo! The best taco bowls are made in Trump Tower Grill. I love the Hispanics! May 5th 2016

2. All of the women on The Apprentice flirted with me - consciously or unconsciously. That's to be expected. *Trump: How to Get Rich 2004*

3. Part of the beauty of me is that I am very rich. ABC's Good Morning America, March 2011.

4. I don't wear a rug—it's mine. And I promise not to talk about your massive plastic surgeries that didn't work. Twitter, 2012 About Cher

5. I like people who weren't captured, I don't like losers. Family Leadership Summit in Ames, Iowa July 18th.

6. If somebody screws you, screw them back in SPADES! *Think Big: 2008*

7. The concept of global warming was created by and for the Chinese in order to make U.S. manufacturing non-competitive." DJT Tweet, November 2012.

8. I wouldn't mind a little bow. In Japan, they bow. I love it. Only thing I love about Japan. Washington Post, September 2004

9. When I think I'm right, nothing bothers me. Nothing gets too much under my skin. 60 Minutes Interview 1985.

10. I have a great relationship with the blacks. Albany's Talk Radio 1300, 2011.

11. I mean, you know, when you're asking me about who's running this, this this, that's not, that is not, I will be so good at the military, your head will spin. Hugh Hewitt, September 2015.

12. Sorry losers and haters, but my I.Q. is one of the highest -and you all know it! Please don't feel so stupid or insecure, it's not your fault. DJT Twitter, May 2013.

13. The fake media tried to stop us from going to the White House. But I'm president and they're not. John F. Kennedy Center for the Performing Arts. July 2017.

14. There is something on that birth certificate — maybe religion, maybe it says he's a Muslim, I don't know. Fox News, Bill O'Reilly 2011.

15. Bing bing, bong bong, bing bing bing. August 2015. Michigan

16. Hillary's a very smart woman, very tough woman, that's fine. She's also a very nice person. I think she's gonna go down at a minimum as a great senator. TV Channel NY1 interview, 2008

17. How stupid are the people of Iowa? How stupid are the people of the country to believe this crap? Iowa Central Community College on Nov. 12, 2015 in Fort Dodge, Iowa.

18. Russia, if you're listening. July 2016.

19. I was in Moscow a couple of months ago, I own the Miss Universe Pageant and they treated me so great. Putin even sent me a present, a beautiful present. 2013

20. He's running his country, and at least he's a leader. Unlike what we have in this country. MSNBC Morning Joe, December 2015.

21. She does have a very nice figure. I've said that if Ivanka weren't my daughter, perhaps I'd be dating her. *The View*, 2006.

22. So obviously, he's a pretty smart cookie. Face The Nation, April 30th, 2017.

23. Do you mind if I sit back a little? Because your breath is very bad—it really is. 1989 appearance on CNN's Larry King Live.

24. In the second grade I actually gave a teacher a black eye —I punched my music teacher because I didn't think he knew anything about music and I almost got expelled. The Art of the Deal, 1987.

25. I won New Hampshire because New Hampshire is a drug-infested den.. Call to Mexican President Enrique Peña Nieto. January 2017.

26. If you see somebody getting ready to throw a tomato, knock the crap out of them. Cedar Rapids, Iowa February 1, 2016.

27 The new Pope is a humble man, very much like me, which probably explains why I like him so much. DJT Tweet December 25, 2013.

28. Writing my inaugural address at the Winter White House, Mar-a-Lago. DJT Twitter, Jan 2017.

29. It would take an hour and a half to learn everything there is to learn about missiles. ... I think I know most of it anyway. Washington Post 1984.

30. That White House is a real dump. *Golf* Magazine, 2017.

31. We're going to win bigly. South Bend, Indiana, May 2016.

32. "North Korea best not make any more threats to the United States. They will be met with fire and fury like the world has never seen" Trump National Golf Club in Bedminster, New Jersey, August 8th, 2017.

DONALD J. TRUMP
45ᵀᴴ PRESIDENT OF THE UNITED STATES
Coloring Book

Other works by S. Eileen Montaño
Find them on Amazon

U.S. PRESIDENTS *Coloring Book*
Enjoy fun facts while coloring all 44 Presidents. Then tear them out and put
them on your wall for easy reference while studying history.

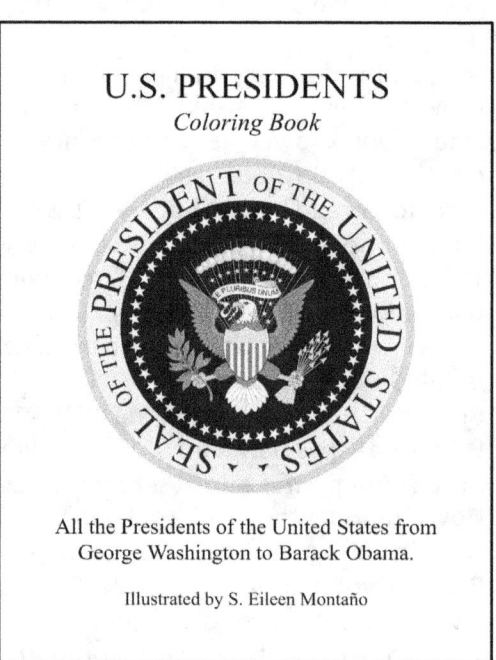

U.S. PRESIDENTS
Coloring Book

All the Presidents of the United States from
George Washington to Barack Obama.

Illustrated by S. Eileen Montaño

WOW

Life from the point
of view of a very
special cat. It's about
friendship, being kind,
appreciative and love.
Colored pencil and
watercolor
illustrations

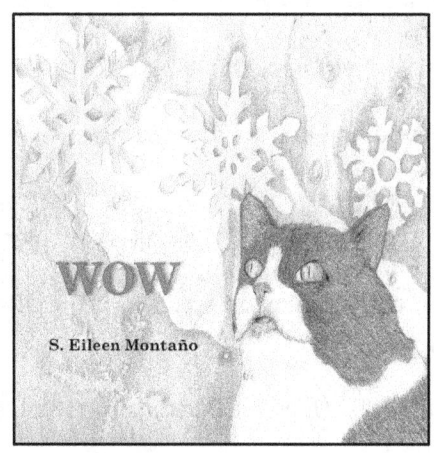

WOW

S. Eileen Montaño

Simply Butterflies

This Color Me Coloring Book is for anyone who
appreciates the beauty of butterflies.

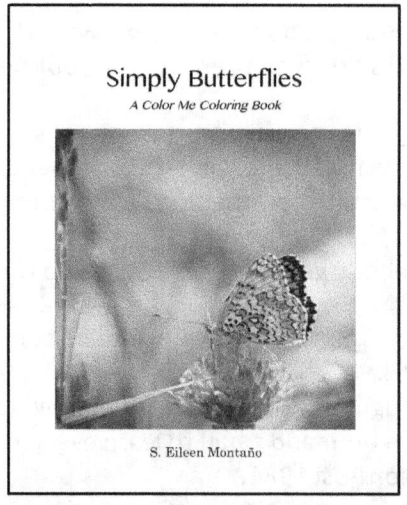

Simply Butterflies
A Color Me Coloring Book

S. Eileen Montaño

www.ingramcontent.com/pod-product-compliance
Lightning Source LLC
Chambersburg PA
CBHW081648220526
45468CB00009B/2591